Emotional Intelligence in the Classroom

The secret of happy teachers

Melinde Coetzee

Cecelia A. Jansen

Emotional Intelligence in the Classroom
First published 2007 by Juta & Co
Mercury Crescent
Wetton, 7780
Cape Town, South Africa

© 2007 Juta

ISBN 978 07021 72 649

All rights reserved. No part of this publication may be reproduced or transmitted in any form or by any means, electronic or mechanical, including photocopying, recording, or any information storage or retrieval system, without permission in writing from the publisher.

Typeset in 10.5/13 Euclid

Project manager: Melanie Wagner
Editor and Proofreader: Lorraine Johnstone
Typesetter: Lebone Publishing Services
Cover designer: WaterBerry CC
Cover artwork: Guy Stubbs
Printed in South Africa by Shumani Printers

The authors and the publisher have made every effort to obtain permission for and to acknowledge the use of copyright material. Should any infringement of copyright have occurred, please contact the publisher, and every effort will be made to rectify omissions or errors in the event of a reprint or new edition.

Foreword

Professor Mandla Makhanya
Executive Dean: College of Human Sciences,
University of South Africa

Teaching continues to be one of the most challenging jobs in the world, in that it situates the teacher in an environment where the act of teaching itself can either make or break the children he or she is tasked to teach. This is a profound statement, as teaching can only thrive if the teacher loves the job that she or he is doing. Teaching is a job that can yield inner satisfaction if the one who does it exudes contentment from within. This love and contentment are indicative of a conducive teaching and learning environment, where the student's self is nurtured. This cannot happen if the teacher is unable to appeal to the inner being of the child. This inner being is what I like to refer to as a pliable person inside a person. The inner being has the capacity to shape, since it influences the teacher and the teaching process itself. It has the capacity of being shaped if the content of what is deposited within the person causes her or him to blossom into a "new" being.

I am deeply moved by the overall direction of this book which, as I see it, is towards bringing forth a "balanced" student. This is articulated clearly in the manner in which the authors, Professor Melinde Coetzee and Professor Cecilia Jansen, have packaged it. From the first to the last chapter, the authors have attempted to strike a balance between the act of teaching itself and its reference point, that is, the student. This is what I find exciting in this book, because it posits the effect of the act on the authors.

Learning is an active process of engagement, in which both the student and the teacher should be in a position to learn and unlearn. Learning will take place in many instances when the environment in the classroom is conducive to learning. We tend to regard the well-resourced classroom as a conducive environment for learning, and in doing so we unfortunately forget about the cardinal resource that, above all, is responsible for learning. This cardinal resource is the teacher who has acquired the proper training and understands his or her role as that of guiding a student to success. The learning process takes place when the encounter between the teacher and the student results in a situation where they are both inspired to share their knowledge. The unlearning process takes place when what they already know prior to their encounter is consciously subjected to scrutiny with a view to providing an enriching classroom experience.

Learning should be fun! This is (or should be) inherent in the process of learning. This means that both teachers and learners derive satisfaction from the process of learning. This satisfaction arises from the dialogical process which is a prerequisite for learning. It is through this interaction that the basis of learning is nurtured and this is manifested by the level of understanding that exists between the teacher and the learner. This, in essence, is what this book on emotional intelligence represents.

I encourage all the teachers, student teachers, parents and policy-makers in education to tap into the narrative that is presented to us by these two authors in order to appreciate what I view as the *raison d'être* of teaching. I urge all teachers, without exception, to use this book to recharge their energy whenever they prepare their lesson plans and whenever they prepare themselves to go to school. I believe that decoding its print will immediately help teachers to understand that their work is that of an intimate co-partner in the development of students en route to realising their full potential.

Preface

"A teacher takes a hand, opens a mind and touches a heart."

As a self-help manual, this book is intended to introduce educators, and in particular undergraduate students in the education field, to the concept of emotional intelligence as it relates to the classroom context. Emotional intelligence forms a critical aspect of the curriculum for the development of educators. Emotional intelligence entails the intelligence that all successful educators bring to their daily interactions with learners.

Throughout the years successful educators have known that effective communication, treating their learners with dignity and respect, and modelling appropriate behaviour can create a high nurturance classroom climate. Such a climate fosters learner and teacher self-esteem, initiative, motivation, satisfaction in teaching and learning, and overall academic performance levels.

Emotionally intelligent behaviour emerges when teachers acquire those attitudes and skills that enable them to cope more effectively with the daily challenges presented by the classroom environment and their personal lives.

Emotional intelligence as a concept covers a broad domain, so condensing it into a book of this format was a daunting task. However, teachers (and adults from all walks of life) will find this *primer* on emotional intelligence easy to follow. More importantly, they will find it filled with ideas on how to use emotional intelligence wisely in their own life and, of course, in the classroom environment. The secret to emotional intelligence lies in wanting to work on it one step at a time.

Use this book as a workbook and a personal guide to more effective and satisfactory learner interaction and teaching practices. As individuals, you will find particular areas with which to start your own development plan to optimise your role as educators. However, adopting new behaviours and attitudes takes much longer than a quick read through the book.

Developing our emotional intelligence is a lifelong process. As unique individuals, we are worth the effort! Deepening the self-knowledge of our emotional awareness and developing the skills to use our emotional life for achieving greater satisfaction in life will help us to live out the secret of being truly happy teachers, that is, in an emotional landscape filled with the inner peace and vitality that create a fulfilling life lived in joy.

Professor Melinde Coetzee
Tel: +27 12 429 8204
Mobile: 083 500 8621
E-mail: coetzm1@unisa.ac.za

Professor Cecelia A. Jansen
Tel: +27 12 429 4070
Mobile: 083 400 2907/8
E-mail: janseca@unisa.ac.za

Contents

Foreword   iii

Preface   iv

Chapter 1
Teaching is a work of heart   1

Chapter 2
Taking a closer look at emotions   12

Chapter 3
Kindling warmth in the classroom   30

Chapter 4
The power of managing emotions   49

Chapter 5
Nurturing the child that hurts   75

Chapter 6
Be good to yourself   93

Chapter 7
Do it ... because you can!   110

Appendix
The behavioural profile of effective teachers   137

Bibliography   139

Glossary of terms   143

Index   151

Dedication

For all our teachers whose dedication to our children blesses the world with a rainbow of Love ...

"You deserve a banner of blessing, a standing ovation, a grand declaration for being a teacher so very special. You're forever inspiring, always desiring to instill within the heart of each child a love of learning."
(Karla Dornacher)

"Thank you for making our child love school because he loved his teacher."
(Parent feedback at the end of a school year to Laura Schultz – a teacher ahead of her time)

Acknowledgement

We would like to express our sincerest gratitude to Steve Biddulph whose highly acclaimed *The Secret of Happy Children* inspired the concept of this book. We truly believe that by guiding our teachers to heal their emotional selves, the classroom can become a healing context in which our children will thrive and grow.

Chapter 1

Teaching is a work of heart

In chapter 1, we take a closer look at the teacher's role in creating classroom conditions that promote the growth and performance of learners. The turbulence of our time draws heightened attention to the importance of helping both children and adults to grow socially and emotionally. Although the primary responsibility for children's social and emotional education devolves onto the family, changes in family structures, such as divorce, separation and single parenthood, as well as other adverse socio-economic conditions, increasingly deprive children of resources for socio-emotional support.

The school environment, with its emphasis on the teacher as secondary educator, is a critically important means for providing the conditions and experiences required for learners to perform at a higher intellectual level. Without compromising academic integrity, the school environment is challenged to develop social skills in learners that enable them to deal with their emotional needs for security and a sense of belonging. Unless the emotional needs of children are met, they cannot function effectively and derive the intellectual benefit of their education. The emotional state of both teachers and learners affects the children's attention, focus, perception, the time spent on tasks and their academic performance.

Teachers who demonstrate emotionally intelligent behaviour in the classroom are more effective in achieving the academic goals they have set for themselves. Emotionally intelligent teachers convey a sense of caring towards their learners. They create an emotional climate that enhances the learning environment, reduces peer conflict and facilitates a more desirable teaching context.

Effective teachers exert a significant impact on children's achievements, emotions and development. (Elizabeth Morris)

The term 'emotional intelligence' was originally coined by Peter Salovey and John D. Mayer (1990) to complement the traditional view of general intelligence. Emotional intelligence emphasises behaviour that requires emotional and behavioural control in social situations. Although the construct is still in a stage of active development, researchers agree that:

The secret of happy teachers

- Emotional intelligence is distinct from but positively related to other intelligences. More specifically, it is regarded as the intelligence that people apply to their emotional lives.
- Emotional intelligence is an individual difference in the sense that some people are more endowed than others.
- Emotional intelligence develops over a person's lifespan and can be enhanced through training and practice.
- Emotional intelligence involves particular abilities to reason intelligently about emotions, including identifying and perceiving emotion (in oneself and others), as well as the skills to understand and reflectively manage those emotions.

At the heart of emotional intelligence lies the ability to sustain an optimistic outlook in life, a healthy self-esteem and qualities such as self-appreciation, self-respect, intuition, character, integrity and motivation. It includes good communication and relationship skills.

Emotionally intelligent teachers are recognised by their happy disposition and optimism towards their profession and life in general. Happy teachers display ten characteristics:

1. They have a *deep desire* to know and experience who they really are and what they can become through their innate ability to choose who they want to be.
2. They cultivate an *attitude* of openness, love and acceptance towards their daily experiences.
3. They are sincerely *grateful* for the blessings and opportunities life brings. They approach life and their profession with *optimism*. They strive to discover the beauty and richness of life at each new moment.
4. They view their *relationships* with others as *sacred*. For happy teachers relationships are life's grand opportunity to create and produce the experience of being their best.
5. They have chosen teaching as a *profession* because it provides them with opportunities to experience who they are and what they can become by serving others. They have a passion for stimulating and activating the hearts and minds of their young and inexperienced learners.
6. They are deeply *passionate* about giving of their best in the spirit of co-operation, enthusiasm and love. They ask: "How can I best serve my learners and the community?" "What can I give them today?" "What can I do to be the best possible teacher today?"
7. They regard teaching as an *opportunity to serve* others to the best of their ability without being world famous leaders or accomplishing great deeds to make contribution to humanity. They realise that the more they put their

heart into serving others, the greater and more fulfilling their teaching and personal lives will become.
8. They are *efficient, considerate and conscious* as they go about their teaching and daily interactions. They teach with an attitude of joy, harmony and co-operation.
9. They make their *own life a priority*. They honour themselves in all that they think, do and say. They make an effort to bring balance to their own life first. They know that the greatest gift they can give their learners (and others) is the example of their own harmonious life.
10. They openly express their *genuine care* for their learners. They know that the learners will perform to the best of their ability in an environment where they feel physically and emotionally safe. They consistently set and uphold clearly defined *boundaries* in a gentle but assertive manner.

These characteristics are the traits of emotionally intelligent teachers. Emotional intelligence refers to an array of attitudes, social skills and a personal management style that allow us to succeed in the teaching profession and life in general.

No job competes with the responsibility of shaping and moulding a new human being. (James C. Dobson)

Teaching with emotional intelligence

It is hard to deny that teachers are often emotionally overwhelmed with having to meet the expectations and demands set by the education system, parents, colleagues and learners. However, the onus remains on the teacher to deliberately decide to serve the teaching profession with pride, compassion and passion. Teachers give meaning to their chosen profession and make a difference in children's lives when they accept these challenges and the opportunities they present.

Teachers who are able to display emotionally intelligent behaviour towards their learners activate and nourish the hearts of their learners. Emotional intelligence creates the conditions that help learners feel they are cared for by someone who accepts them unconditionally and respects their uniqueness. Such teachers set clearly defined boundaries which are consistently upheld. They involve learners in classroom activities and make them feel they belong. An emotionally intelligent teacher will encourage learners to take an active part in classroom decision-making.

Emotional intelligence develops the knowledge and skills needed for teachers to create a classroom climate that can calm learners down. Learners become motivated when they are approached with respect, genuineness and empathy.

Words of encouragement create incredible support for learners. When children feel content and safe in the classroom, they are more motivated to learn and perform. The learning

Emotional Intelligence in the Classroom

> *Level with a child by being honest. Nobody spots a phony quicker than a child.*
> (May MacCracken)

experience is joyful and leads to the teacher feeling satisfied that a contribution has been made to the quality of some child's life. To empower another human being with knowledge, skills and the inspiration to grow is indeed an act of the heart. It reflects a deep and sincere belief in the potential of others.

Emotionally intelligent teachers have the ability to ignite or enkindle a passionate heart and a questing mind within themselves. This makes a critical difference in the emotional environment of the classroom. By demonstrating emotionally intelligent behaviour, teachers model values and behaviour that teach young minds social and emotional management skills.

Teachers need to create a psychologically safe space where learners feel respected and understood. This helps learners to do the inner listening required for them to become attuned to the language of their own physical state and the emotional changes which allow their self-awareness to blossom.

> *Your greatest pleasure is that which rebounds from hearts that you have made glad.*
> (Henry Ward Beecher)

Children learn to absorb the skills of communication and negotiation. When they acquire the subtle skills of knowing themselves well enough, they are able to manage their own energy states in a warm, nurturing classroom atmosphere.

It's all a matter of self-esteem

Researchers like Robert Reasoner (1992) and Nathaniel Branden (1994) view the development of a healthy self-esteem in children as central to their emotional functioning and their ability to have healthy interactions with others. Self-esteem evolves in response to kindness and appreciation. This means that the developing child must be treated with empathy, genuineness and respect. When children feel physically and emotionally safe, their self-esteem unfolds.

For many children school represents a second chance in the sense that they have another opportunity to acquire a better self-esteem and a better vision of life than that offered at home. Nathaniel Branden (1994) indicates that a teacher who projects confidence in a child's competence and goodness is a powerful antidote to a family where such confidence is lacking.

Research conducted by Robert Reasoner (1992) and Nathanial Branden (1994) indicates that the conditions that underpin the healthy emotional development of children include being cared for by someone who:
- loves and likes them and who can express this;
- gives them clearly defined boundaries which are consistently upheld; and
- allows them to take an active part in decision-making.

Low self-esteem

Teachers who lack self-esteem find it hard to display emotionally intelligent behaviour. They tend to be teachers who do not inspire, but humiliate. Their language is marked by ridicule and sarcasm rather than courtesy, dignity and respect. They make invidious comparisons whereby they flatter one learner at the expense of another. Their impatience is often unmanaged as they give way to anger, thus deepening the learners' fear of making mistakes. Their notions of discipline revolve around threats of pain. They have not learned to motivate and inspire children by modelling positive values. Instead they evoke fear and lower the self-esteem of their learners.

A low self-esteem in children leads to an inner emotional landscape that is the seedbed for fear-based feelings: fear of being rejected, abandoned, unworthy, inadequate or not good enough. Fear-based feelings make children withdraw from classroom activities. Their mental state becomes characterised by an inability to study and concentrate. They are depressed, detached and confused.

Behaviour generated by a low self-esteem in teachers has a profound impact on the emotional climate in the classroom. Emotional climate can be understood as the specific atmosphere that has a significant bearing on learners' attitude and willingness to learn (see chapter 3).

Fortunately, most teachers do want to make a positive contribution to the minds of those entrusted to their care. If they sometimes do harm, it is not intentional, but rather because of their own inability to manage their emotional responses successfully.

Emotionally intelligent behaviour in teachers is not about making learners feel good about themselves all the time. It is not about praising and applauding learners for anything and everything; nor is it about dismissing the importance of objective accomplishments and handing out gold stars on every possible occasion. This would only serve to propound the mistaken notion of entitlement and divorce self-esteem from healthy behaviour and good character.

The essence of developing a healthy self-esteem in learners is to treat them in ways that help them to trust their own minds and let them know that they are worthy of happiness. Effective teaching is about getting learners to gain a healthy self-esteem. Self-esteem nourishes eight core aspects in learners:

1. their ability to think;
2. their ability to deal creatively with the basic challenges of life;

Believe in other people even if they don't believe in themselves. Listen to them and empathise with them. Help them to affirm their positive traits. (Stephen R. Covey)

3. the right to be successful and happy;
4. a feeling of being worthy and deserving;
5. the right to dignity;
6. the right to assert their needs and wants;
7. the right to achieve their goals; and
8. the right to enjoy the fruits of their efforts.

How self-esteem influences emotional intelligence

Emotions are the primary motivating forces that arouse, direct and sustain our daily activities and interactions with others. Emotional intelligence is important for our emotional well-being, our happiness and our social interaction with others. Emotional intelligence describes the extent to which we are able to tap into our feelings and emotions:

- as a source of energy to guide our thinking and actions;
- to achieve our personal goals in life; and
- to solve problems.

In literature, feelings are often referred to as the language of the soul. In teaching, feelings may also be regarded as the language of the heart. To know what is true for ourselves about any issue, we need only look at how we *feel* about it. After that we can apply our thinking to reason about our feelings and emotions. Thinking is the ability to discern between feelings and to determine what the feelings are telling us about an experience and our response. Our rational minds help us to reason intelligently about our emotions. They help us to achieve our goals in life and to behave in ways that are beneficial rather than harmful to ourselves and others.

Emotional intelligence is about being able to balance the rational and emotional aspects of our minds. The secret of happy teachers is that they trust their minds, judgements and feelings. If we trust all three, we are more likely to operate as thinking and feeling beings.

High self-esteem

When we exercise our ability to think and truly feel, we bring an appropriate awareness to our thoughts, beliefs and needs. We start to recognise how they influence our emotional response to events, situations and people. Self-awareness, in turn, regulates our thoughts and emotions insofar as they enable us to behave in a socially responsible manner. Our self-respect grows and we make others feel safe in our presence. In addition, our own self-esteem (positive thoughts, beliefs and feelings about ourselves) is reinforced.

If we distrust our thoughts and feelings, we are more likely to be mentally passive. We are less aware of our emotions and how our emotions could lead us to respond in ways that are harmful to ourselves and others. When our actions generate disappointing or painful results, we feel justified in distrusting our thoughts and feelings, and thus ourselves.

A high self-esteem leads us to think positively about our abilities. We feel good about ourselves and are motivated to achieve our goals in life. This makes us more likely to persist in the face of difficulty. On the other hand, a low self-esteem could tempt us to give up easily or to go through the motions of trying without really giving of our best, simply because we think and feel negatively about ourselves.

Research conducted by Bandura (1997) shows that people with a high self-esteem persist at a task for significantly longer than people with a low self-esteem. Perseverance makes the likelihood of success higher than the likelihood of failure. Without perseverance the chances are that we will fail more often than we succeed. Either way, success or failure, our view about our feelings and ourselves will be reinforced.

Self-respect elicits respect from others. If we respect ourselves, we expect others to deal with us respectfully. We send out signals and behave in ways that increase the likelihood of others responding appropriately. When they do, we are reinforced and confirmed in our initial belief that we are worthy of respect. In turn, this belief will help us to treat others with respect. Consequently, respect becomes a value by which we live.

On the other hand, lack of self-respect leads to an acceptance of discourtesy, abuse or exploitation from others. A person who lacks self-respect unconsciously transmits this to other people who then treat them at their own self-estimate. When this happens, they submit to ill-treatment and their self-respect deteriorates even more. People with little self-respect will tend to treat others with a lack of respect. Consequently, it becomes a value of how to treat others because they believe that they themselves (and thus other people) are not worthy of respect.

The value of developing a healthy self-esteem as a core aspect of emotional intelligence does not merely lie in the fact that it allows us to *feel* better; it also allows us to *live* better. This is because we tend to respond to challenges and opportunities more resourcefully and more appropriately. A healthy self-esteem enables us to behave in an emotionally intelligent way, and vice versa, emotional intelligence leads to a healthier self-esteem.

There are positive correlations between a healthy self-esteem and the traits of emotionally intelligent behaviour

Have you ever noticed that being with some people makes you feel happier, while interaction with others leads to your feeling anxious, depressed or angry? (McQuaid and Carmona)

that have a direct bearing on our capacity for achievement and happiness. Healthy self-esteem correlates with rationality, realism, intuitiveness, creativity, independence, flexibility, an ability to manage change, a willingness to admit (and correct) mistakes, benevolence and co-operative behaviour.

Poor self-esteem correlates with irrationality, blindness to reality, rigidity, fear of the new and unfamiliar, inappropriate conformity or inappropriate rebelliousness, defensiveness, overcompliance, or conversely, overcontrolling behaviour and fear of or hostility towards others. These traits usually lead to socially irresponsible behaviour towards ourselves and others.

Nathaniel Branden (1994) writes that with a more solid self-esteem we are better equipped to cope with troubles that arise in our personal lives and careers. Also we are quicker to pick ourselves up after a fall and have more energy to begin anew. A higher self-esteem makes us more likely to seek challenging and demanding goals in terms of what we hope to experience in life, whether this is emotionally, intellectually, creatively or spiritually.

Words make a powerful impact and they're not easily forgotten. Wounds inflicted by words of anger or hate can last a very long time. (Brian L. Weiss)

People with a high self-esteem tend to be open, honest and appropriate in their communications. They believe their thoughts have value. They tend to form nourishing relationships, where they treat others with respect, benevolence, goodwill and fairness. These are all behavioural values that help to create an emotionally warm classroom atmosphere. They indicate that the teacher feels good about himself or herself.

In conclusion, happy teachers realise the value of improving their emotional intelligence in their daily interactions. They are committed to raising their own level of conscious awareness. They bring responsibility and integrity to the classroom environment and to their dealings with other people.

In chapter 2 we take a look at emotions and explore our emotional literacy. Emotional literacy is at the heart of developing emotional intelligence.

Teaching is a work of heart

> **Try this now!**
>
> Think back to a time when you felt really valued and worthwhile, even if it was only for a short time. Then try to remember a time when you felt devalued and worthless. Try to capture the fullness of both experiences.
>
> Look at this scale running from 1 to 10: 1 signifies feelings of worthlessness and 10 signifies feelings of value.
>
> Review the experiences of the past day or week. Use the scale to rate your level of self-esteem in each situation.
>
>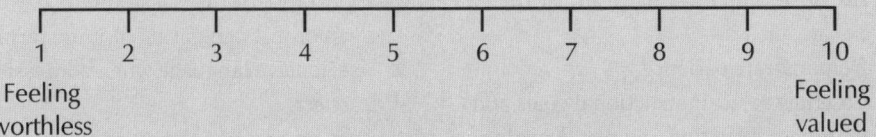
>
> 1 2 3 4 5 6 7 8 9 10
> Feeling worthless — Feeling valued
>
> - What does this show you about your general level of self-respect and how you value yourself?
> - Does your rating correspond with what you believe about your own value and how you experience your worth?
>
> Imagine your learners are watching you in the classroom. Write up a list of all your behaviours, traits, qualities and attitudes that your learners observe.
>
> - Which items on the list would you like to have known (those you take delight in)?
> - Which items on the list would you not like to have known (those you keep quiet about and find most difficult to accept)?
> - How do you feel when your unpleasant side is exposed and how do you react?
> - How do your beliefs about your worth and value influence the way you feel about and treat your learners?

Table 1.1 Characteristics of teacher self-esteem in the classroom

Teachers with a healthy self-esteem	Teachers with a poor self-esteem
■ Exude an aura of authority and affection. ■ Take pride in their physical appearance, dress neatly and professionally, serve as a role model to learners. ■ Use humour to create a warm, friendly atmosphere where learners open up. ■ Are humble, yet assertive and elicit respect from learners. ■ Are confident, realistic and honest in their interaction with learners. ■ Understand human behaviour and childhood development.	■ Punish learners. ■ Do not care about their physical appearance, dress in a sloppy, untidy way. ■ Create an emotional distance by being strict, authoritarian, cold and impersonal towards learners. ■ Are arrogant and aggressive towards learners, elicit fear and disrespect. ■ Display less patience in their instruction. ■ Show less empathy for children with problems. ■ Engage in less effective problem-solving. ■ Are more critical of their learners.

- Understand the unique differences between children's learning abilities and pace of learning.
- Monitor learner progress closely.
- Provide feedback to learners about progress and achievements.
- Are willing to examine their own behaviour objectively.
- Are willing to learn new skills.
- Are flexible and willing to adjust their behaviour.
- Demonstrate patience.
- Carefully select instructional goals and materials, structure and plan learning activities.
- Involve learners in the learning process and classroom activities.
- Maintain discipline and set safe boundaries.
- Involve learners in creating a clean and inspiring classroom environment that they feel proud of.
- Develop creative methods to motivate learners to perform.
- Respond to the learning and emotional needs of learners.
- Minimise disruptions in the classroom.
- Maximise learners' educational experience.

- Provide less positive feedback to learners.
- Complain frequently about having to deal with undisciplined and unmotivated learners.
- Use terms such as obedience, laying down the law, being tough.
- Focus on learners' areas of weakness.
- Emphasise learners' lack of effort.
- Do not pay attention to the physical appearance of the classroom (e.g. whether clean or dirty, inspiring or uninspiring).
- Use abusive language when addressing learners.
- Keep an emotional distance and are not available for learners with learning or emotional problems.

Taking action!

Three suggestions for putting the ideas in this chapter into practice:

1. Gain a deeper understanding of the unique emotional needs of the learners in your classroom. What is their socio-emotional background? Try to obtain more information about their social circumstances. Examine how these may influence their behaviour in the classroom. How would you describe your current level of self-esteem? Can you think of ways to improve your level of self-esteem?
2. Think deeply about why you have chosen teaching as a profession. Be honest with yourself. Have you chosen teaching because you are passionate about serving others with your own unique talent? Have you chosen this profession because of your ability to teach, or merely because it is a form of employment? Your answer to these questions will explain why you look forward to interacting with your learners or why you shy away from having to face them on yet another day.
3. Make a commitment to learn more about emotional intelligence. Think about how you can improve your skills and abilities so as to interact with your learners and other people in healthier ways. By working through this book, you can become a happier teacher. Remember, you are worth it.

Review questions

1. Describe the characteristics of emotionally intelligent teachers. How do these characteristics contribute towards the learning and growth of your class?
2. Why is it important for teachers to develop their emotional intelligence?
3. How does the self-esteem of teachers influence the way they feel about and treat their learners?
4. How can teachers help their learners to develop a healthy self-esteem? Why is it important for children and teachers to develop a healthy self-esteem?
5. How does self-esteem influence emotional intelligence?
6. Compare the characteristics of teachers with a healthy self-esteem to those of teachers with a low self-esteem.
7. What are your beliefs about the role teachers play in creating a high nurturance and emotionally warm classroom atmosphere?

In a snapshot

1. Effective teachers exert a significant impact on their learners' achievement, emotions and socio-emotional development.
2. Happy teachers have developed distinctive characteristics that make them successful in their profession.
3. A healthy self-esteem is at the core of our emotional functioning and our ability to develop effective social relationships.
4. Emotionally intelligent teachers are aware of the unique socio-emotional needs of their learners.
5. At the heart of effective teaching lies the ability of teachers to build up a healthy self-esteem in their learners.
6. Self-esteem influences our ability to demonstrate emotionally intelligent behaviour.

Suggested reading

Bandura, A. (1997) *Self-efficacy in Changing Societies.* Cambridge: Cambridge University Press

Branden, N. (1994) *Six Pillars of Self-esteem.* New York: Bantam

Reasoner, RW. (1992) *Building Self-esteem in Elementary Schools.* Palo Alto, California: Consulting Psychologists Press

Saarni, C. (1997) 'Emotional competence and self-regulation in childhood' in P. Salovey & DJ. Sluyter (editors) *Emotional Development and Emotional Intelligence: Educational Implications.* New York: Basic Books

Saarni, C. (1999) *The Development of Emotional Competence.* New York: Guilford

Chapter 2  Taking a closer look at emotions

In chapter 1, we described the role of the teacher in creating those conditions which promote the growth and performance of their learners. We explored the importance of a healthy self-esteem as being central to emotionally intelligent behaviour in the classroom. In this chapter, we take a closer look at what emotions are and the role they play in our own lives. We look at how the teacher's emotions impact on the classroom.

A happy teacher is the secret to creating an optimal teaching and learning environment. However, being a teacher who is continually happy is not necessarily ideal. Teachers who are in touch with their feelings and who know how to negotiate their way through life's myriad feelings have found the secret to the inner peace and vitality that make up emotional health. Reuven Bar-On's international research on emotional intelligence (1997) reveals that people who are satisfied with their lives, genuinely enjoy the company of others. They derive pleasure from life, are pleasant and have a happy disposition.

Happy people feel good and at ease in both work and leisure. They let their hair down and enjoy having fun. In this sense, happy teachers radiate a general feeling of cheerfulness and enthusiasm. These are barometric indicators of their overall degree of emotional intelligence and emotional functioning.

It takes two people to have an ego battle. But it only takes one happy person to create the peace and love that bring warmth and safety to the heart of another. (Melinde Coetzee)

What are emotions?

You are sitting at your desk reviewing an outline of the curriculum you have planned for your learners. You have filled it with exciting lessons to make the day a very interesting learning opportunity. You are probably not aware of any strong feelings in yourself. You know you are feeling optimistic. You are calm about the day ahead of you. The school bell rings. You hear children laughing and running to the classroom. One of the boys starts a fight with another before entering the classroom. Immediately, you become aware that you are no longer calm. Your heart is pounding. There is a knot in your stomach. Your breathing is quicker. You know you are feeling anxious and upset. Your mood has changed.

We carry our emotions in our minds. Emotions are energy in motion (e + motion = emotion). Emotion is what you *do* with the feelings you have. A feeling is simply a thought that you have, whereas an emotion is an eruption, an expression of that thought in a particular way. Emotion makes the thought real by putting it into action. Our thoughts, however slight they may be, are always brushed with feeling. For example, this may happen at the level of mood (gloom, excitement, anxiety) while we consider what to do next. Our thoughts and beliefs about an event, situation or person trigger particular feelings, such as fear, excitement, anxiety or anger. This is illustrated in table 2.1.

Table 2.1 Examples of thoughts brushed with feeling

Experience	Thought	Feeling
object (e.g. gun)	"It's dangerous."	fear
situation	"It's going to be tough teaching today."	anxiety
person	"He likes me."	excitement
event	"The children are open and receptive today."	contentment

The information gathered through our five senses (sight, hearing, smell, taste and touch) is interpreted in terms of our beliefs, assumptions, values and previous experiences. The process is not conscious and happens very quickly. To a large extent, the way we interpret (think about) the information we receive determines how we feel about it. For example, when the teacher hears the noisy way in which the children are approaching the classroom or the fight happening between the two boys.

In *What God Wants* (2005) Neale Donald Walsch explains that the mind does not know a thing about feelings, only the heart does. The mind thinks it knows and so it responds to its interpretation of the information gathered from the five senses. According to this view, emotion can be regarded as that which the mind tells the body to *do* about its feelings. We feel something and then get emotional about it. Feelings move energy around within us; hence, we are full of energy in motion.

Choose how you feel

We can consciously choose *how* to feel. Feelings create our inner reality, and that inner reality creates our outer experiences. We can control our feelings by controlling our interpretation of the information received via the body. We can also control what we *do* with the feeling, that is, our reaction or noticeable behaviour. When we think before we *react*, it helps us to

I've heard people say that they learned the truth of health and wholeness by being sick, the reality of abundance by suffering lack, the beauty of harmonious relationships by witnessing first hand the ugliness of discord. If that's the game plan they have chosen, fine. But doesn't it remind you of the old joke about someone who hit himself on the head with a hammer, so it would feel good when he stopped? Many of us do that. Why can't we accept the fact that positive living is the natural way – that this is a totally benevolent universe? (John Price) respond in more creative ways to information presented by the situation or person confronting us.

We always have a choice about how we want to behave. We are surrounded by energy in motion, that is, our own thoughts and feelings and those of others. They flow around and past us like a current. The more we become aware of our own state of mind and how it affects our mood or the way we react to the behaviour of others, the less outside events, situations or people's behaviour will affect us.

Being in touch with our own feelings helps us to remain heart-centred and to regulate our own thoughts and feelings. It enables us to *respond* in ways that increase our own personal happiness because we *consciously choose* to behave in a socially responsible manner towards ourselves and others.

The secret of why we have emotions

In *The Manager's Pocket Guide to Emotional Intelligence* (2000) Emily Sterret explains that recent research shows emotions to be a result of brain chemistry. These conclusions come from neuroscience, evolution, medicine and psychology. Emotional signals in the brain are felt throughout the body, for example, in the gut, the heart, the head, the neck and shoulders. These sensations are vital signals: if we learn to read them, they can help us make responsible decisions and initiate actions that promote our safety, well-being and success in life.

The brain is regarded as having three functional layers:
1. a *brain stem* (first brain) located just above the spinal cord, which tells our lungs to breathe and our hearts to beat;
2. the *limbic system* or *emotional brain*, which is thought to have developed out of the brain stem; and
3. the *rational (thinking) brain* or the *neocortex*, which enables us to comprehend sensory information and to plan accordingly.

The brain stem (first brain) is the seat of autonomic or automatic response, as well as the seat of habits. It connects us to our external world through our senses (sight, hearing, smell, taste and touch). It controls the recognised impulses and passes them along to the two higher brain levels. The limbic system (emotional brain) in humans is located approximately at the centre of the brain (midbrain). It is made up of the amygdale, the hippocampus and other structures. Scientists believe that the limbic system is the control centre for emotions.

The limbic system stores every experience we have from the first moments of life. These impressions are stored there long before we acquire verbal or higher thinking abilities to express them in words. This vast warehouse of feelings and impressions in the limbic system provides a context (or meaning) for our memories. Messages are transmitted to the brain by neurons that travel through the electrical transmission system of nerves, as well as by the body's chemical system. This system is based on chemicals called peptides, which have receptors in every cell of the body. These highly sensitive information substances are thought to be the chemical substrates of emotion. They trigger impressions and memories throughout our lives. The three parts of the brain are linked to all body systems and the peptides are responsible for the emotions felt in different parts of the body.

When information enters the limbic system, the body experiences sensations, transmitted by the peptides or chemical information substances in the form of a reaction to the stimulus. The rational brain (neocortex) assists us with functions related to thinking and language: planning, questioning, making decisions, solving problems and generating new ideas. Millions of connections link the neocortex to the limbic system (emotional brain). This allows the emotional and the thinking brains to influence one another and provide rich data from which to draw conclusions and initiate action.

Emily Sterret (2000) maintains that our emotions have helped us immeasurably over the course of human evolution. Emotional responses are milliseconds faster than cognitive (thinking) responses. The lightning fast reactions that bypass the rational brain centre were often survival responses for our distant ancestors. Today, physical survival is less under threat, yet the data from the emotional brain still give important clues to our surroundings and the action we need to take. Deliberately ignoring this data leaves us with only partial information. It is important to know how to use and regulate this information to the benefit of our emotional well-being.

According to Neale Donald Walsch (2005) feelings are a valuable tool of the brain that most people do not use effectively. Many people spend their lives *reacting* to feelings rather than *creating* them. One of the greatest secrets of a balanced emotional life is the ability to create feelings *inside* of ourselves that can facilitate events *outside* of ourselves. This is possible because feelings move energy around, and energy is the essence of life.

Now is important

Eckart Tolle's book *The Power of Now* (2001) shows how we are all extraordinary creators. Tolle highlights the importance of the present moment in what he calls *Now*. We create our reality at every single moment of Now, making that Now the most important moment that there is. Neale Donald Walsch (2005) points out that it is not what we *do* in the moment of Now that is the most important element of the creative process, but how we *feel*. Our feelings create our inner reality, and our inner reality creates our outer experience.

The fact that we can create something by picturing it in our minds, by seeing it as already accomplished, and by allowing ourselves to experience the *feeling* associated with it, is evidence of one of the greatest secrets of happy teachers. They realise that they may have any feeling they desire, simply by deciding how they feel about the experience they are having. They exercise their ability to choose at that moment that they will experience something in a new way. For example, a teacher can look at an anticipated event in life or in the classroom, and decide beforehand how he or she is going to feel about it. This enables the teacher to create a new perception about what is going on right here, right now in the classroom. Neale Donald Walsch (2005) reminds us that the secret is that feelings can be *chosen*. They do not have to be *endured*. When functioning well, our emotions can:

- help us find out what we want and what is right for us;
- tell us if something needs changing in ourselves, others and the world;
- help us communicate our priorities and needs to others;
- help us empathise with other people and with ourselves;
- warn us of danger;
- motivate us to grow; and
- help us clarify our own values so as to guide us.

The ability to choose our feelings is a core secret of emotional intelligence in the classroom (see chapter 4). Developing emotional intelligence helps teachers to create day-to-day, moment-to-moment experiences in the classroom by learning the skill of consciously deciding how to choose to feel about the behaviour of learners or events. Emotional intelligence skills help teachers to *consciously decide* how *to choose to express* any feeling, whether the feeling arose deliberately or not.

Emotions that impact on the classroom atmosphere

Generally, emotions are described as four basic feelings: anger, fear, sadness and joy, with all other feelings being a combination of these. Some researchers in emotion make a distinction between pleasure and pain in terms of the past, present and future. Others recognise love and fear as the only feelings we have with all other feelings being shades of love and fear. What is important is to realise that we experience a mixture of feelings. For example, jealousy is a mixture of anger and fear; whereas joy is a mixture of gratitude and love.

In her book *Spiritual Growth* (1989), Sanya Roman points out that we all have what she refers to as a *birth emotion*. The birth emotion is an innate feeling that we carry with us throughout our lives. It becomes the *feeling tone* for our experiences. Some of us have optimism, happiness or complacency as our main feeling tone, in contrast to people who have an underlying feeling of pessimism, resentment or disappointment. Some people have an easy-going nature, while others are quiet, melancholy, lonely or unhappy. The range of feeling tones include love, seriousness, fun-loving, smugness, superiority, unworthiness and inferiority.

Besides a prominent feeling tone, each person has five to seven satellite emotions that make up his or her primary emotional identity. These emotions are the lenses through which we look at the world. A happy person sees the world differently to an angry or sad person. The experience of each emotion is like putting on a new pair of glasses; every feeling presents a different way of looking at the world. We choose these emotions because they give us the perspective that provides the most growth for us personally (Roman, 1988).

Although our thoughts and beliefs act as triggers for the feelings we experience, at times we also experience emotional reactions, such as the joy of being deeply into a task, for example, a lecture we enjoy, or other pleasure or pain feelings that are not always clearly related to our thoughts and beliefs. We are specifically interested in those feelings that have a profound impact on the emotional climate in the classroom, that have a significant impact on the learners' attitude and their willingness to learn. The classroom climate can be sensed by teachers and learners alike and is assessed according to the learners' and teachers' response to it. The emotional climate in the classroom is created by the teacher.

> **! Try this now!**
>
> Think for a moment about your most prominent feeling. Even if you cannot identify your most noticeable feeling tone right now, know that you do have one.
> - Are you normally happy, easy-going or optimistic?
> - Are you tense, worried or often unhappy?
> - Can you identify the five to seven satellite emotions that make up your very own prime emotional identity?
> - Can you pinpoint the one emotion that you would call your feeling tone?
> - How do your beliefs about your worth and value influence the way you feel about and treat your learners?

The experiences of negative emotions by teachers and learners make inroads on their classroom performance. Negative emotions, such as fear, anxiety, anger, frustration, sadness, depression, detachment, confusion, shame and distraction create mental states that are harmful to performance or attempts at improvement. They also create a cold classroom atmosphere which slows down teaching and learning, adversely affects performance, and ultimately, perpetuates a negative cycle that lowers self-esteem.

On the other hand, positive emotions such as appreciation, joy, happiness, achievement, motivation, relaxation, confidence, engagement, faith, pride and enthusiasm create a safe and loving space characterised by emotional security. Experiences of positive emotions create the conditions for an emotionally warm classroom atmosphere whereby learners motivate themselves, feel good about themselves and expect to succeed. Chapters 3 and 4 respectively demonstrate that the secret of an emotionally warm climate lies in how teachers feel about themselves and their own emotional intelligence.

A teacher who nurtures positive feelings about himself or herself and also the learners can create a healing atmosphere that is more powerful than the negative emotional climate created by the learners' behaviour, feelings, thoughts and attitudes. Steve Biddulph (1999) in *The Secret of Happy Children* says that this is because a growing child learns to deal with feelings socially and has to find constructive outlets for the powerful energy that feelings create. A child depends on adults for this information. The key to happier interactions with learners is being able to understand our own feelings: why we have them, how they can be best expressed and what to avoid.

This book focuses on the key feelings of *love* and *fear*, and their related feelings of joy, compassion, optimism, enthusiasm, gratitude, hope and happiness (love); and anger, anxiety, doubt, sadness, depression and guilt (fear). These emotions determine the general atmosphere in the classroom. They have a profound impact on learners' attitude and their willingness to learn and engage in classroom activities. Let's take a closer look at these emotions.

Love

In *Omni Reveals the Four Principles of Creation* (2001), John Payne defines love as the complete and total acceptance of what is. Our greatest longing is for *unconditional* love. We all seek to accept others and allow them to be who they are. We also desire to accept and allow ourselves to be who we are. The will to love unconditionally is deeply embedded in our hearts.

Our will to love draws us automatically towards the state of unconditional love, which is a state of *allowing*. The will to love cannot be denied. We cannot resist it and we cannot flee from it, even if we pretend not to have it or act as if it were not there. It is possible to fully experience a range of feelings or a reality that seems devoid of love, yet the will to love unconditionally draws us forward in our development. It stimulates us to grow and express ourselves in ever-expanding and creative ways.

Unconditional love is indeed the very breath of life. Without it we live at the periphery of our own possibilities, unable to understand who or what we are. Only with a full realisation of love can we truly awaken to life and its expansion. Gratitude, hope, trust, compassion, forgiveness and joy are all heartfelt qualities of unconditional love that allow us to feel happy. Payne (2001) refers to four key emotions (see table 2.2) that hold the secret to true happiness: self-appreciation, allowing, gratitude and forgiveness.

> *The love we express – whether it's a neighbour, a child or a sweetheart – reflects the love we have for ourselves and our world as a whole. Genuine love is an attitude of our heart.*
> *(Jan Denise)*

Table 2.2 The four secrets of happiness

Emotion	How it increases happiness
Self-appreciation	Enhances our ability to create through the acknowledgement of our natural talents and abilities.
Allowing	Is the key to living a life full of unconditional love.
Gratitude	Makes us magnetic to abundance in all areas of our lives, what we focus on increases.
Forgiveness (of self and others)	Leads to health and well-being, to feeling happy about ourselves, life and other people. If you are unwell, there is always something to forgive, first about yourself and then others.

Worthiness

Emotional intelligence allows us to tap into the energy of love, particularly love of self. It enables us to create or generate feelings that are energising and make us feel good about ourselves, our life and our purpose in life. We must first learn to regard ourselves as worthy before we can see this in others. Worthiness means we respect ourselves. Self-respect entails expectations of friendship, love, kindness and happiness as a natural result of who we are and what we do.

Nathanial Branden (1994) reminds us that self-respect is the inner conviction of our own value. It is not a delusion of being perfect or superior to everyone else. It is the knowledge that our own life and well-being are worth acting on to support, protect

Anger is simply the cry we make when we push pain from ourselves. Pain turned outward breeds emotions such as hate, anger and jealousy. When we turn our pain outward, we look for someone or something to attach blame to. (Lynn Atkinson)

and nurture; that we are good and worthwhile and therefore deserving of the respect of others; that our happiness and personal fulfillment are important enough to work towards.

Fear

Fear exists as heavy emotion, as a weight or a feeling of tension in the body. It can hide in busy-ness and rushing around, parading under the guise of productivity, of doing rather than being. There are moments when we feel light and full of joy, and there are moments when we do not. These heavier moments are often an indication of fear.

Fear must be faced directly. Avoiding it will not make it go away because whatever we resist will persist. For example, if you feel fear and insist, "I am not afraid – everything is fine," you will become more frightened, not less. The way to dispel fear completely is to admit, "I'm scared – I'm really frightened!" Another way to dispel fear is with humour, for example, remind yourself of fear's acronym: fear is nothing but **F**alse **E**vidence **A**ppearing as **R**eal.

Fear can be faced and transformed by breathing relaxation into the body. When you sense a feeling you do not like, face it. Suspend judgement, do not try to interpret what it means to you. Stop to see if you can notice something beautiful about the situation, event or person. Thinking positive, healing thoughts are always more powerful than negative ones.

! Try this now!

Call to mind an incident where you were angry with someone. Remember all the details of the event. Describe it literally to yourself. Visualise it and experience the feeling of anger fully. Notice the bodily sensations that go with it.

- What is happening, for example, with your arms, your neck and shoulder muscles, your eyes, your breathing, posture and pulse?
- What do you notice about what you did with your anger?
- What were the accompanying symptoms and words?
- Is this a familiar pattern?
- How do you feel now? Are you satisfied or do you feel you need to change?

How do your beliefs about your worth and value influence the way you feel about and treat your learners?

Repeat the exercise for different emotions, such as fear, grief, happiness, boredom or embarrassment. This will give you an overview of how you manage your emotions.

Feelings lose their power if we do not resist them and willingly go through the experience. When we freely let go, we create a new, empowering, healing experience. Beneath *anger* lies emotional pain, such as hurt, pride, shame, frustration, sadness, terror or fear. Anger represents energy in motion from the suppression of pain. Not allowing anger to flow is like putting a cap on a volcano; one day it will erupt. The secret is to *feel* the emotion, not talk about it, not analyse it, not label it, but truly experience it. The next step is to love it, embrace it and, finally, let it go.

Guilt

Guilt makes us feel bad about ourselves for perceived mistakes that we *think* we have made. Our feelings of guilt may be likened to a doomsday sentence that puts our bodies at great discomfort. We sense danger. Guilt always expects a reprimand. It does not rest until punishment occurs. This expectation creates a negative mindset whereby we expect punishment. We scan the horizon of daily life expecting to find punishment.

Our feelings create our outside reality; we actually create and attract one negative situation after another because we think we deserve the pain in our lives. The secret is to forgive ourselves for the mistakes we think we have made. Forgiveness puts an end to our self-created suffering. Forgiveness helps us to return to appreciating ourselves for who we are. When we let go of our guilt, we start to feel happy again.

Helplessness and depression

Feelings of *helplessness* and *depression* occur when we think we have no hope or way out of a situation. Often we go to our minds and try to talk ourselves out of the depression, only to find discouragement. When our minds are depressed, we tend to think that our bodies have to be depressed too. We consume pills to knock our bodies out. We lay our bodies down and try to forget about them. What we need to remember is that it is not our bodies that are depressed, but our minds. We can relieve the problem when we start moving our bodies into a new, enlivened state by engaging, for example, in creative forms of self-expression, like dancing to music or going for a walk in nature.

When our bodies delight in themselves, we reach a point where we can pull ourselves out of the depression. When we find ourselves in state of mental difficulty, the worst thing to do is compound that state by throwing the body into it as well. It is better to pull the body out of the dilemma, to claim the wonder of its vigour and life, and to start working with what we have. Like all things, depression comes and goes.

The fountainhead of love is within your own heart. Don't look to others to provide the love you need. Love comes from our willingness to think loving thoughts, experience loving feelings (such as joy and gratitude) and act in trusting love-inspired ways. If you are willing to do this, your cup will run over. You will constantly have the love that you need, and you will take delight in offering it to others.
(Paul Ferrini)

*The work that remains to be done begins on the **inside** and ends up having an impact on the **outside**.*

The secret is to keep reminding ourselves that our feelings are the effect of attaching our minds to a prior belief. We think, experience a feeling, and then act on that feeling in an attempt to alter it. When we attempt to alter our feelings, we reach outside ourselves to relationships, food, alcohol and drugs for temporary comfort. Instead what we need to do is change our thoughts about ourselves, our lives, other people, situations and events. When we do this, we transform our lives in the process to a new order of creation, namely: **Think-Feel-Act-Have**.

Happiness anxiety

Happiness anxiety is very common. Happiness can activate subversive internal voices that say, "I don't deserve this" or "It will never last". Such thoughts are based on our fear of being wrong or rejected by others simply because we feel happy. We need to develop the courage to tolerate our happy feelings without succumbing to self-sabotage until such time as we lose our fear of happiness and realise that it will not destroy us.

Our feelings of love or fear create a set of implicit expectations about what is possible and appropriate to us. These expectations generate actions that turn into realities that confirm and strengthen the original beliefs. We call this cycle a self-fulfilling prophecy.

Self-fulfilling prophecies are based upon our self-concept: who and what we consciously and subconsciously think we are. Our physical and psychological traits, assets and liabilities, our possibilities and limitations all make up our self-concept. To understand a person's behaviour we need to understand the self-concept behind it. The self-concept includes our level of self-esteem, but is more global.

Many people tend to sabotage themselves at the height of success. This happens when success clashes with implicit beliefs about what is appropriate to us. If our self-concept cannot accommodate a given level success and if our self-concept does not change, then the chances are we will fall prey to self-sabotage.

Developing our emotional intelligence helps us to change our thoughts, beliefs and feelings about ourselves. Not only does it help us to develop a healthier self-esteem, but as our sense of emotional well-being increases, our self-concept changes and we learn to stop behaviours that self-sabotage. Simply put, we learn to manage our happiness anxiety and success anxiety. As we learn to appreciate ourselves more, we allow ourselves both happiness and success.

The role of feelings in creating the classroom climate

We often forget how much our lives are controlled by our emotions of fear, doubt, anxiety and anger. Once we shift our focus of attention from fear-based feelings to emotions of love, gratitude, joy, peace and calm, we will be able to make more positive choices for ourselves. Feelings are energy in motion created by the minds of the people in the classroom. Therefore, they can be felt in the *atmosphere* of the classroom. For example, when a teacher walks into a classroom where learners have been having an argument, even if the argument stops the moment the teacher enters, he or she can still feel the negative energy. The teacher will experience and interpret the atmosphere as being full of bad vibes.

This happens because the feeling, that is, the energy, is concentrated in space. It creates vibrations that are sensed by the teacher and the learners. The teacher's thoughts about the negative energy, that is, his or her *interpretation* of the energy, will determine his or her response towards the learners. This affects the *emotional climate* of the classroom. Ultimately, the thoughts of the teacher and his or her emotional responses are at the centre of what occurs within the classroom.

Everything in the Universe, whether solid, liquid or gas, and including our emotions, thoughts and actions, is vibrating energy. This is known as the Law of Vibration. Norma Milanovich and Shirley McCune (1996) write in *The Light Shall Set You Free* that our personal vibrations not only affect others, they also act like a magnet to attract in equal measure similar vibrations. For instance, angry, cynical or pessimistic thoughts or emotions tend to attract, in equal measure, people and/or circumstances with similar vibrations. Happily, the same is true for loving and positive thoughts or emotions. Therefore, it is we ourselves who create our own lives and the healthy interactions we have with learners and other people.

Just as light and sound have a range of vibrations from low to high, so too do our thoughts and emotions. Fear-based thoughts and emotions are at the low end of the scale, while love-based thoughts and emotions vibrate at the high end of the emotional scale. Higher vibrations transmute lower vibrations, and thereby automatically raise our vibration. Thus, we benefit directly through increases in love, power, wisdom and physical well-being.

Medical research has also discovered the effects of the Law of Vibration. Research results show how happiness promotes health and well-being, while unhappiness destroys it. The reasons are that happy thoughts and feelings have high vibrations, while negative ones, like depression, anger or anxiety, have much lower vibrations.

Awareness of your body, thoughts, and emotions allows you to discover the effect other people have on you.
(S. Roman)

The classroom atmosphere is only mirroring to you the feelings you have about yourself.

The implications of this are that if we increase our overall vibration, lower vibrations would automatically be transmuted. It means that people, situations or circumstances with lower vibrations would not disturb us. In other words, the higher our vibration, the greater our health and well-being. It is really as simple as that.

The way to raise our vibration is by developing emotional intelligence so that we become more aware of our emotions and more self-confident in regulating them (see chapter 4). This will promote our health and well-being and create fulfilling and healthy interpersonal relations with others.

> **Try this now!**
>
> For a moment, think back on your day. You probably experienced many different feelings ranging from high, happy, positive thoughts and experiences to feelings of anger, frustration, anxiety or depression. Some of your feelings were reactions to the people you were with.
>
> - What feelings did you have today?
> - How did you feel with certain people or with your learners in the classroom?
>
> Become aware of your body when you are with a particular person or a specific group of children in your classroom. Your body gives you clues about how you are handling people.
>
> - Are you hunched over or are you up straight?
> - Are your arms folded in front of you or at the back of you, leaving your heart open?
>
> For the next week, notice how you feel with each person or group of learners that you come into contact with. Pay attention to your feelings. You may not feel as if you are being affected by them until you take a deeper look at what is happening to your feelings and to your body.
>
> How do your beliefs about your worth and value influence the way you feel about and treat your learners?

Roman (1988) tells us that people can make us feel tired, or happy and energised, or drained and depressed, or anxious and angry, even though ten minutes earlier we felt calm and optimistic. Do not blame yourself when you feel depleted by other people. Just be aware of your feelings, your thoughts and your body. Often we pick up the thoughts and feelings of those around us.

When you lean forward, you give away your energy and push in on your learners' space. When you lean way back, you avoid their energy, and they come at you too strongly. When you sit or stand up straight, with your shoulders square, you are in most of your personal power. That is a position of balance and centredness which allows you to control the energy around you. With both feet flat on the floor, your body breathing rhythmically and your shoulders square, you can tap into your inner voice that helps you without fail to make better choices.

Happy teachers tune in to and manage the classroom atmosphere. You cannot have a healthy, warm connection with your learners or others if you see yourself as wrong. If you feel bad about yourself or a relationship, tell yourself: "I am perfect as I am." Then look deeper into yourself, check in with yourself and ask: "Do I feel good? Do I feel confident, positive, or am I feeling inadequate, negative?" When you feel depreciated, angry or drained it is a sign that your learners are not open to your energy. Every interaction, tough as it may be, only tells you something about yourself. As you look into yourself and listen to your feelings and body, you realise that you are probably undervaluing or depreciating yourself in some way. The classroom atmosphere will mirror to you the feelings you have about yourself.

Being a teacher requires us to give more energy than we receive. Self-beliefs, such as "I am not deserving", can close up and deplete energy. Your learners' feelings will awaken in you your matching emotions through the principle of resonance. As you calm your emotions through techniques, such as deep breathing or taking a walk, you will be able to handle strong emotions in the classroom.

How do you calm your emotions? Listen to the slightly negative feelings within you before they create a crisis. When you begin to notice situations that are undervaluing you, or demanding too much of you, *clear the negative energy within you first*. Remain up straight and strong and centred in your body. Do not lean forward or backward. When you are with learners who drain you, learn to *put your feelings into words*, even if only to yourself. Putting your feelings into words is a very powerful way to cleanse other people's energy from your space. Do not express anger to the learners, but do get it out of your system. Always *breathe deeply*. Breath calms the mind and emotions. It relaxes the body and allows you to tap into your wiser inner self. Simply become aware of the sounds or the smells in the room and the energy interaction at a level beyond words. Monitor how you feel. Observe what is being said to you and how the learners behave. You will find a wealth of information flowing to you.

Roman (1988) admonishes to *always make yourself your first priority*. Make a commitment to listen to your feelings from moment to moment. Acknowledge that you have enough sense of self to do what is appropriate and socially responsible in the present moment. If you do not make your life, thoughts, goals and time a priority, you may become lost in the currents of other people's or learners' desires and expectations. If you know who you are, trust in yourself, make your life a priority, acknowledge your feelings and act upon them from a place of calmness. You can choose how to respond in a way that honours yourself and your learners more deeply.

Blind spots in sensing the classroom atmosphere

One of the biggest blind spots in sensing the classroom atmosphere is being too aware of ourselves, that is, existing too much at the centre stage of our lives. We are blocked from sensing our learners' needs and moods when we are more concerned with what others think about us than with what we can do to nurture and assist them (which, of course, will in turn nurture and assist us).

Often teachers feel they are actors on a stage, with everybody else (learners, parents, colleagues) watching them and judging them. However, it is we ourselves who have put us on stage, we ourselves watching, observing and judging us. When we do this, we feel unduly responsible for other people, such as our learners: if they do not perform or feel bad then we may feel we have caused it.

We can remove our blind spots by changing our perspective. From time to time, put yourself in your learners' shoes. Try to see your life through their eyes. Consider their challenges, attitudes and socio-emotional needs. Let these images flow through your mind. When you take time to step outside of your own life and viewpoint, you will begin to understand your learners' behaviour and moods. You will also sense your own feelings and thoughts more clearly.

Emily Sterrett (2000) maintains that success in social interactions is the hallmark of emotional intelligence. We need to develop the ability to accurately assess other people and to respond accordingly. The first step towards skillful social behaviour is social knowledge or awareness. Such awareness or the ability to tune in to others and to feel what they are feeling is called *empathy*. Without empathy we have difficulty sustaining healthy relationships.

Empathy is our capacity to understand and share other people's emotions without losing the awareness of our own. When we are able to empathise with our learners, we are sensitive towards their emotional needs. We are able to temporarily identify with their lives and share their ideas and emotions, we are open to their points of view. Empathy helps us to relate in an emotionally healthy manner to the needs of our learners. However, empathy requires patience, sensitivity, openness and a ready *willingness* to truly understand. The secret is to give our learners what we would like to receive:

You are always in relationship, and I am not talking about love affairs. They are only a small part of relationship. I am talking about life, about relating to everyone you see. Every moment of your day, when you are in the presence of another, you have the opportunity to increase your movement towards more positive living ... What happens then is you increase your vibration and release "Love" energy into the atmosphere around you. (Bartholomew) love, support, appreciation, healing and acknowledgement; and we will get it back from them.

Teachers who are able to empathise ask themselves questions like:
- "Do I try to understand why Mary is lately so quick tempered and refuses to do her homework?"
- "Why has Patrick isolated himself from class activities?"

They do so in an effort to make emotional contact with their learners. They also use their body language and will look into the learner's eyes, stand still and listen attentively to what the learner has to say. This shows the learner that the teacher is truly interested and willing to understand.

> **Try this now!**
>
> Start today. Look at the reality that your learners live in. See the stress they are under and the kinds of thoughts that go through their minds. Observe what their needs are. With this understanding your interaction will be healing and nurturing for you and them.
>
> Make this process a habit. Then, when you are concerned with what your learners think of you, or what is happening to them, use the same process to sense their mood, your own mood and the emotional climate in the classroom.
>
> How do your beliefs about your worth and value influence the way you feel about and treat your learners?

Creating healthy connections

Healthy connections with our learners start from the awareness of any resentment we may have towards them now, any feelings of superiority or inferiority, any grudge, any negative thoughts we have sent their way, even if it is only a perception that something about them is not up to our standard.

To connect in a healthy way with our learners, we need to forgive ourselves for anything we have sent their way at a thought or emotional level that has not assisted their growth. We need to ask how our communication can promote their personal growth. We need to find ways to show we appreciate and acknowledge them.

To do so, we must first put ourselves in their shoes and leave the narrow focus of our own personality and selves. This challenges us to let go of a right-wrong way of thinking. When you observe a quality or characteristic in your learners that you do not like, find out how it fits into their life. Look at how that particular trait works for them.

Apart from the ability to empathise, teachers also need to be *compassionate*. Compassion is a way for teachers to reach out to their learners when they are hurting. Compassion makes learners feel cared for, seen, felt, known and not alone. Compassion is healing.

If you want others to be happy, practise compassion. If you want to be happy, practise compassion. (Dalai Lama)

If you have been betrayed, you can either decide that you cannot trust anyone or you can continue to take leaps of faith. You choose to stop being afraid of the consequences of trusting someone and to start connecting deeply with that person instead. Ultimately, trust requires you to move towards love and away from fear.
(Rikki Robbins)

As people we have a need for authentic emotional connection. For us teachers, this could mean that we set aside the agenda for the day, put down the memo we were reading and focus on the person we are with. Compassion is the willingness to drop what we are engaged in and to attend to another person's real feelings, longings, aspirations and pain in the moment. This readiness will alter the felt connection between our learners and us forever.

In this chapter, we discussed emotions and how our thoughts and feelings create our realities. We also took a closer look at how the teacher's moods and emotions impact on the classroom climate. As we open ourselves up to the full range of experiences within ourselves, we become aware of what we perceive in each moment and no longer deny some feelings while clinging to others. By knowing our own pain, we build a bridge towards the pain of others. This enables us to step out of our self-absorption and to offer help. When we actually understand how it feels to be suffering, in ourselves and in others, we are compelled to live in a way that creates as little harm as possible.

Taking action!

Four suggestions for putting the ideas in this chapter into practice:

1. Think about your most prominent feeling tone, the core feeling that you carried with you for most of your life. How does this feeling influence the way you approach life in general? How does this feeling influence your thoughts about your learners and your daily interaction with them? What feelings, such as confidence, love, courage or compassion, would now benefit your growth the most? Think of this quality and imagine yourself demonstrating it in a future situation. How would this quality change your learners' behaviour?

2. For the next week, notice how you feel with each person or the group of learners you come in contact with. Pay attention to your feelings. Write them down in a journal. How did your mood change since waking up in the morning and during the day? Which feelings created a positive atmosphere in the classroom? Which feelings created a negative atmosphere?

3. Forgive yourself for any negative thoughts you have had about yourself or your learners or any other person in your life. Forgive yourself for anything you have sent their way at a thought or emotional level that has not nurtured their growth.

4. Take one day where you focus wholly on looking at the reality your learners live in, the stress they are under, the thoughts that go through their minds and what their needs are. Write down in a journal the images that come to mind. What can you do to help them grow and feel cared for?

Review questions

1. Explain emotions and feelings. How are they triggered in our bodies?
2. Explain the reasons that human beings have a feeling nature.
3. How do emotions impact on the classroom atmosphere? What role do the emotions of teachers play?
4. Describe how the primary emotions influence our interactions with others.
5. What are the blind spots in sensing the classroom atmosphere?
6. Explain the importance of empathy and compassion in the classroom.
7. What can teachers do to establish healthy connections with their learners?

✓ In a snapshot

1. Happy teachers are in touch with their feelings. They know how to negotiate their way through the feelings that life brings.
2. Emotions can be used and regulated to create lives and interpersonal relationships that promote our emotional well-being and sense of inner satisfaction.
3. Our feelings create our inner reality, and our inner reality creates our outer experience.
4. The teacher's thoughts and emotions have a profound impact on the classroom atmosphere.
5. Positive emotions are more powerful than negative emotions.
6. Teachers who are too self-absorbed have difficulty in sensing the classroom atmosphere. By developing our empathy and compassion we are able to overcome our blind spots and foster healthy connections with our learners.

Suggested reading

Biddulph, S. (1999) *The Secret of Happy Children*. New York: Harper-Collins

Morris, E. (2002) 'Emotional literacy training for educators: Developing the whole person – linking hearts and minds in all learners' *Gifted Education International*, 16: 133–137

Salovey, P. & Mayer, JD. (1990) 'Emotional intelligence' *Imagination, Cognition, and Personality*, 9: 185–211

Sterret, EA. (2000) *The Manager's Pocket Guide to Emotional Intelligence*. Amherst, MA: HRD Press

Tolle, E. (2001) *Practising the Power of Now*. London: Hodder & Stoughton

Walsch, ND. (2005) *What God Wants: A Compelling Answer to Humanity's Biggest Question*. London: Hodder Mobius

Chapter 3 Kindling warmth in the classroom

Chapter 2 explored how the teacher's emotions and feelings influence the classroom environment. In this chapter we will discuss the factors that determine the classroom climate.

To teach is to touch a life forever.

The classroom environment refers to the conditions, circumstances and influences surrounding and affecting the development and performance of learners. These include the physical conditions of the school and classroom, the teacher's physical appearance, body language, language patterns, behaviour and attitude towards learners. To a large extent the personal values of the teacher influence how he or she treats and interacts with the learners. Values are the norms, beliefs, principles and preferences that determine how people in a particular society, community or family behave and relate to each other. Children learn values through the behaviour that adults model. Therefore, the teacher's behaviour models a particular system of values regarding acceptable human interaction. A teacher who shouts and rages at learners sends out the message that it is socially acceptable to treat others in a hostile and disrespectful manner. Similarly, a teacher who treats all learners with courtesy and respect signals to the class that the dignity and feelings of others matter.

The values that teachers model through their behaviour create a particular emotional climate or classroom atmosphere that the learners sense. The classroom climate is the shared perception of learners about the classroom environment. It includes how they think and feel about the way the teacher treats them. The classroom climate can range from a warm, welcoming and nurturing atmosphere to one characterised by coldness and indifference. This is evident in the behaviour that the teacher displays.

The emotional climate in the classroom has a significant impact on the learners' attitude and willingness to learn. In an emotionally warm classroom atmosphere learners feel accepted for their uniqueness. Consequently, their self-esteem is enhanced. A positive learning environment helps to fulfill both the teacher's and learners' emotional needs for psychological safety, unconditional regard and acceptance, the feeling of belonging, purposeful behaviour and a sense of personal competence.

> *Peter lives in a small mining village with good parents who love their children. Peter's father shows his love for his family by generously taking care of their material needs. He finds it very difficult to put his arm around Peter. He never tells his son that he loves him or that he is proud of him. Peter's mother is domineering, controlling and possessive. As the eldest of three children, Peter works very hard to gain acceptance and approval from his parents and teachers. Peter describes his feelings as follows: "I feel incompetent, lonely, totally worthless – and unloved at home."*
>
> *Fortunately, his mathematics teacher praises him often. The simple words spoken by the teacher, "Thanks, Peter"; "Well done, my boy!"; "So kind of you to help me carry these books", usually accompanied by a slight pressure of the hand on his shoulder, motivate Peter to give of his best in the maths class. He feels that the teacher accepts him unconditionally.*

Emotional needs in the classroom

The three primary reasons why children acquire knowledge are generally the love of learning itself, the desire for social relationships, and the desire for practical information to use in solving immediate problems. However, the emotional needs of learners have an impact on their desire to learn. Robert Reasoner (1992) describes five basic emotional needs that must be addressed to create classroom conditions for optimal learning and growth. These are psychological safety, a positive self-image, feelings of belonging, purposeful behaviour and a sense of personal competence.

Psychological safety

The need to feel safe and secure is a basic human psychological need. In the classroom it is achieved when learners know what is expected, feel safe and protected, are able to trust others and are able to anticipate or predict the sequence of events from experience.

When learners come from a dysfunctional family they may feel insecure, for example:
- Their parents may be separated or divorced.
- They may have moved home a number of times.
- They come from a different culture.
- They attended several schools.
- They spend large amounts of time in the care of a variety of adults.
- They are left alone for most of their waking hours.

Learners who feel secure are relatively free from worry and anxiety. They feel comfortable and protected, are more willing to take risks, enter new situations with confidence, are better able to focus their energy on the task at hand.

Learners' need for psychological safety can be addressed by establishing clearly defined classroom procedures, policies and practices. These will reduce anxiety felt by both the teacher and learners. Classroom rules enable learners to perform comfortably in class. Learners should be involved in defining the rules and teachers should apply rules in ways that preserve everyone's self-respect. It is good practice to entrust learners with classroom materials and equipment.

Teachers have to act responsibly and keep learners' secrets and confidences. Psychological safety means behaving consistently so that learners can accurately anticipate and predict what to expect. When teachers respond inconsistently according to the mood they are in, they raise the anxiety level in learners.

When teachers cannot keep commitments, they should offer learners an explanation. This will give the children insight into adult behaviour, actions, frustrations and personal values. Learners are apt to value and respect adults and to behave responsibly when they have teachers who serve as responsible role models.

Research indicates that the physical conditions of the classroom have an impact on motivating children to learn, for example, whether the room is neat, clean and orderly or well-equipped with the necessary resources and facilities. An untidy, dirty school and classroom environment which lacks the basic facilities will lead to learners feeling emotionally unsafe and uninspired. Such an environment reflects a value that sends the disturbing message that it is acceptable to neglect and destroy our surroundings.

Positive self-image

The development of the learners' self-concept begins at an early age. It is based on how the world responds to their efforts to make their needs known.

Feedback from adults is a significant factor in the formation of children's self-concept up until age eight to ten, when they begin to develop a stronger sense of personal awareness. When the feedback is more positive than negative, children develop positive feelings about themselves and generally relate well to others.

Learners with a positive self-image have a realistic view of themselves. They know their strengths and weaknesses. They are aware of how they appear to others. They also feel capable of being loved and entitled to happiness. This is sometimes described as the sense of personal worth or self-respect.

The learners' self-image develops from the rapport established between teacher and learners, which enables all to feel accepted as unique individuals. Learners gain personal respect for themselves when they become aware of their strengths and areas for growth through constructive feedback from the teacher.

A teacher can systematically modify the learners' self-image by honouring each child's uniqueness, fostering a positive self-image, demonstrating acceptance and caring, and building self-awareness of their strengths and weaknesses.

Feelings of belonging

Apart from feeling honoured for their uniqueness, learners need to feel that they are equal to others in the group. It is important for learners to feel they have the same basic qualities as others. The task of the teacher is to help learners realise when it is important for them to act as unique individuals and when it is appropriate for them to act as members of the group.

Feelings of belonging make learners feel part of something larger. They feel accepted and valued as a member of the family, team or culture and develop a healthy sense of pride.

Teachers can increase feelings of belonging by creating an accepting, warm classroom environment. They reduce feelings of isolation by involving learners in class activities and providing them with opportunities to be of service to others. This encourages bonding, class cohesiveness and a sense of group pride.

Purposeful behaviour

Learners need to engage in purposeful behaviour because it brings meaning to their efforts. If their efforts remain directed towards pleasing or complying with the demands of adults, learners lack internal motivation.

It is imperative to develop in learners an intrinsic joy of learning and the achievement of solving their own problems. This not only leads to responsible citizenship but also to feelings of positive self-esteem.

Purposeful behaviour develops when teachers and learners take responsibility for and initiative in the learning process, for example, when teachers set realistic expectations and help their learners to gain confidence in striving for personal achievable goals. Teachers address the learners' need for purposeful behaviour when they convey clear expectations, express confidence and faith in their learners' abilities, strengthen values, such as responsibility, effort, honesty, perseverance, determination, commitment and help learners to set realistic goals.

Personal competence

Personal competence is essential to the development of a healthy self-esteem. Learners develop a sense of personal competence when they believe they can achieve their goals, overcome their problems and achieve the success they dream of.

Personal competence requires the ability to identify options, to make wise choices and decisions, to apply problem-solving skills and to use resources effectively. Learners who possess and apply these skills believe in their own potential for success. As a result, they tend to take responsibility for their behaviour, to demonstrate initiative in solving problems and to be highly motivated to achieve their goals.

Teachers address the need for personal competence when they make learners aware of the alternatives or options available for them to achieve their goals. Teachers need to provide encouragement and support, give constructive feedback and celebrate their learners' success.

A spiralling, cyclical process is set in motion when both teachers and learners achieve success. Both feel more secure when they function effectively within the limits set. Positive self-images are formed and feelings of connectedness through the support of others develop. Learners are willing to set higher goals for themselves. As teachers and learners acquire new skills, they become more proficient at using resources to achieve their goals and start to feel more in control of their lives. Personal competence or efficacy makes the teaching process easier and more productive because learners take greater responsibility for their own learning.

A look filled with understanding, an accepting smile, a loving word, a meal shared in warmth and awareness are the things which create happiness in the present moment.
(Thich Nhat Hanh)

The classroom climate

Figure 3.1 shows the factors that influence the classroom climate. These factors correspond with the basic emotional needs of learners. They can be formally measured by a tool like the *Emotional Climate Sensor*™.

Teacher general demeanour/behavioural style

A behavioural style that displays unconditional acceptance, respect and empathy towards the learners, as well as passion and enthusiasm towards the subject, creates a classroom atmosphere in which learners feel motivated and eager to learn and perform. Learners find it important that teachers set an example in terms of morals and standards. When this happens they develop respect for the teacher.

Other important characteristics are the physical appearance of the teacher (professionally dressed), positive body language (smiling when greeting learners), friendly tone of voice, constructive language patterns, a lively interest in the learners, a positive attitude, optimism, patience, knowledge about the subject and willingness to encourage and provide guidance regarding learning and personal problems.[1]

Psychological safety

Clearly identified classroom procedures, policies and practices reduce anxiety felt by both teacher and learners and creates a sense of psychological safety that enables comfortable performance in the classroom. The physical classroom conditions, such as sufficient facilities, equipment, tidiness and cleanliness also influence learners' motivation and ability to concentrate.

Positive self-image

Learners develop a positive self-image from the rapport established between teacher and learners. They feel accepted as unique individuals and develop self-respect by becoming aware of their strengths and weaknesses.

Feelings of belonging

A sense of belonging or connectedness is gained from engendering an emotionally warm classroom atmosphere where teachers and learners feel they are a part of something larger. As contributing members of a winning team they feel valued and accepted by others.

Purposeful behaviour

A sense of purpose is gained when teachers and learners take responsibility or initiative in the learning process, for example, by setting realistic expectations and by helping learners to gain confidence to strive for personal achievable goals.

Personal competence

Recognition given by the teacher for the accomplishment of goals helps learners to gain a sense of competence.

---

[1] The Behavioural profile of effective teachers is included in the appendix on page 136. The profile is based on extensive research conducted by the authors in school environments of both historically disadvantaged and advantaged learners.

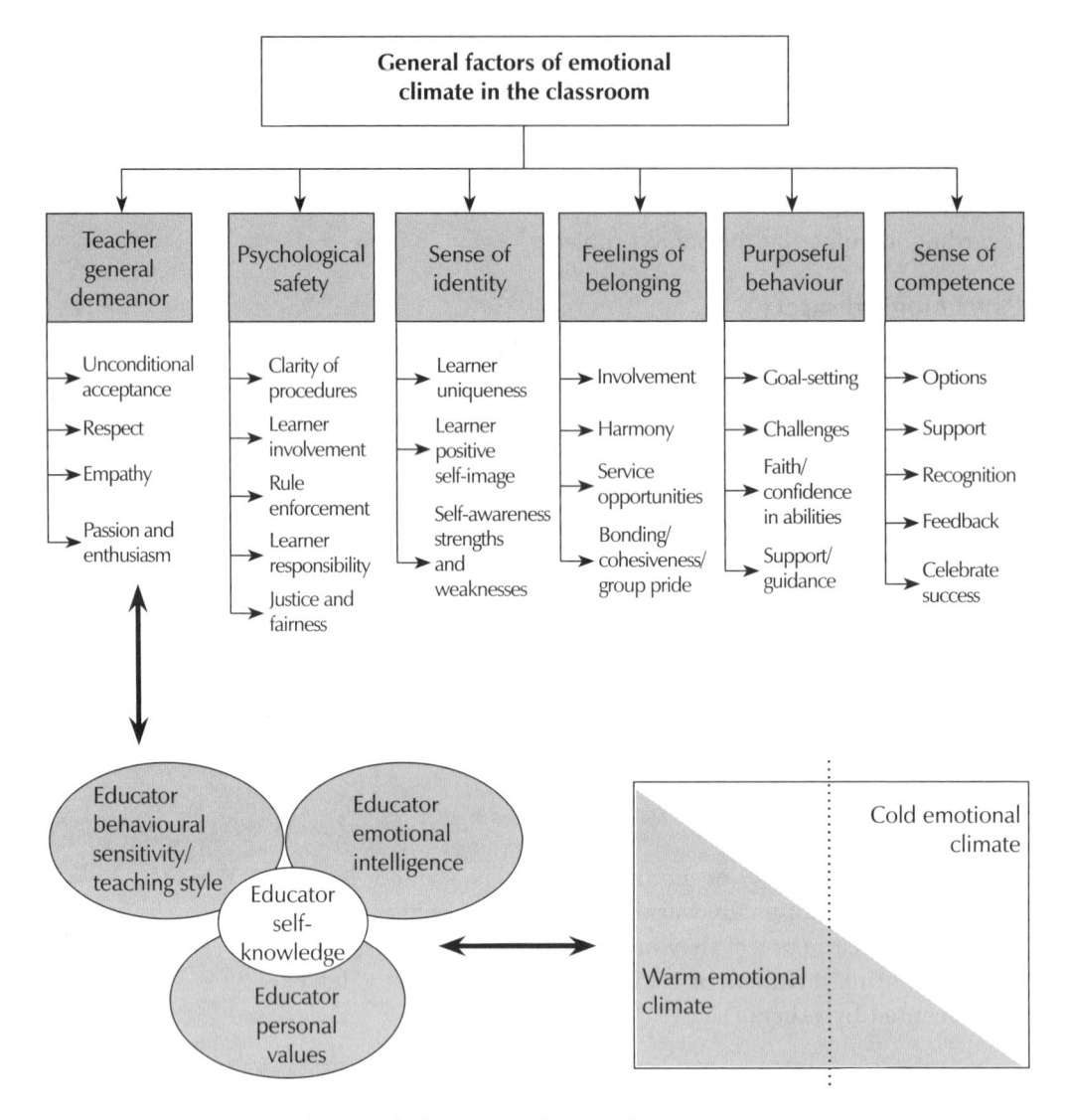

Figure 3.1 Overview of general classroom climate factors

General factors of emotional climate in the classroom

- **Teacher general demeanor**
  - Unconditional acceptance
  - Respect
  - Empathy
  - Passion and enthusiasm

- **Psychological safety**
  - Clarity of procedures
  - Learner involvement
  - Rule enforcement
  - Learner responsibility
  - Justice and fairness

- **Sense of identity**
  - Learner uniqueness
  - Learner positive self-image
  - Self-awareness strengths and weaknesses

- **Feelings of belonging**
  - Involvement
  - Harmony
  - Service opportunities
  - Bonding/cohesiveness/group pride

- **Purposeful behaviour**
  - Goal-setting
  - Challenges
  - Faith/confidence in abilities
  - Support/guidance

- **Sense of competence**
  - Options
  - Support
  - Recognition
  - Feedback
  - Celebrate success

- Educator behavioural sensitivity/teaching style
- Educator emotional intelligence
- Educator self-knowledge
- Educator personal values

- Cold emotional climate
- Warm emotional climate

Teacher's behavioural style

The strength of the classroom climate is related to the teacher's and learners' shared perception of how warm and supportive or how cold, forbidding and punitive the classroom atmosphere is. Research indicates that the behavioural style of the teacher influences the classroom atmosphere and consequently the children's learning and performance.

An emotionally warm behavioural style creates a classroom climate that facilitates optimal learning and performance. An emotionally cold or distant behavioural style slows down teaching and learning and adversely affects the performance of both teacher and learners. The distinctive characteristics of an emotionally warm behavioural style and an emotionally cold behavioural style are summarised in Table 3.1.

Table 3.1 Emotionally warm and emotionally cold behavioural styles

Emotionally warm	Emotionally cold
Real *interest* in the learners results in trust and emotional closeness.	Emotional indifference characterises an attitude of *mistrust* and *coldness* towards learners.
Unconditional acceptance of and *respect* for the learners enables them to feel safe and sheltered in the classroom context.	*Insincerity* and *disrespect* for learners will be characterised by superficial, hostile, vindictive, malicious and aggressive behaviour towards them.
An *optimistic* and *positive attitude* with a sense of *humour* creates a warm and open classroom climate allowing honest communication between teacher and learners.	A *negative outlook* with *closed* and *secretive behaviour* results in an atmosphere of distrust and dishonesty.
Authority exercised in a *reasonable*, *consistent* and *fair* manner demonstrates respect for learners as human beings.	*Authority* used to elicit *submission* inspired by *fear* and *disrespect* for the learners leads to unreasonable and unjust methods to maintain discipline e.g. corporal punishment, abusive shouting.
Cherishing and *embracing* the relationship with the learners results in feelings of mutual goodwill, empathy and co-operation between the teacher and learners.	*No concern* for the relationship with the learners results in disturbed relationships characterised by squabbles and negative criticism.
An understanding of and *empathy* for learners' unique cognitive and emotional needs develops.	*Shows lack of understanding* or *no interest* in the unique cognitive and emotional needs of learners.

Teachers with an emotionally warm style seem to create an emotionally warm classroom atmosphere characterised by feelings of being a close-knit unit with mutual goodwill, empathy and co-operation. The relationship with learners is embraced and cherished.

Teachers with a warm style appear to be aware of learners' cognitive and emotional needs and accept and respect the learners unconditionally. They accept learners for their uniqueness and show an authentic interest in their well-being through open and honest communication. Discipline is handled in a fair, reasonable and consistent manner.

An emotionally warm behavioural style is related to the teacher's ability to demonstrate emotionally intelligent

Most people don't just want soup, they want contact where they are appreciated, loved, feel wanted and find some peace in their hearts. It's the personal touch that matters.
(Sister Dolores)

behaviour in the classroom. Research indicates that the ability to manage emotions makes a positive contribution to the quality of social interactions. Individuals who are socially well-adapted tend to display emotionally intelligent behaviour. They tend to be aware of their own emotions and the impact of their overt behaviour on others. They express their emotions appropriately and are better able to read and respond to the emotions of others. Emotionally intelligent individuals use their emotional and cognitive presence to monitor the socio-emotional climate. They engage in behaviour that facilitates emotional security within themselves and others.

As illustrated in Figure 3.2, self-awareness and intelligent reasoning about our emotions facilitate adaptive responses, a problem-solving approach and constant navigation of our cognitive and affective self-presentation all influence the emotional climate in the classroom. Emotionally intelligent behaviour leads to rapport between teachers and learners, which in turn, facilitates a sense of psychological safety, identity, belonging, purpose and competence.

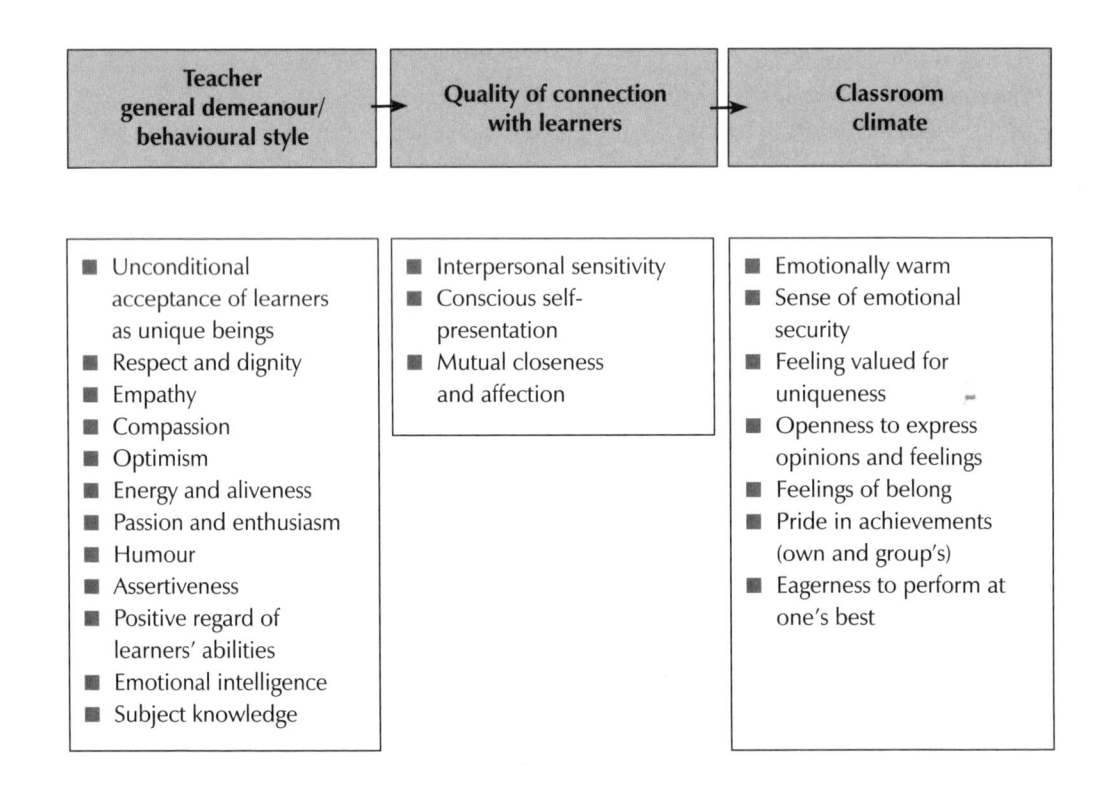

Teacher general demeanour/ behavioural style	Quality of connection with learners	Classroom climate

■ Unconditional acceptance of learners as unique beings ■ Respect and dignity ■ Empathy ■ Compassion ■ Optimism ■ Energy and aliveness ■ Passion and enthusiasm ■ Humour ■ Assertiveness ■ Positive regard of learners' abilities ■ Emotional intelligence ■ Subject knowledge	■ Interpersonal sensitivity ■ Conscious self-presentation ■ Mutual closeness and affection	■ Emotionally warm ■ Sense of emotional security ■ Feeling valued for uniqueness ■ Openness to express opinions and feelings ■ Feelings of belong ■ Pride in achievements (own and group's) ■ Eagerness to perform at one's best

Figure 3.2 Impact of the teacher's behavioural style on classroom climate

The secret of kindling warmth in the classroom

Teachers who are successful in kindling a warm, nurturing classroom atmosphere in which learners feel emotionally safe and motivated, understand the role that their personal values and attitudes play in their ability to demonstrate emotionally intelligent behaviour. Values are relatively permanent ideals and ideas that influence and shape the general nature of our behaviour. *Affiliative* values place a high priority on constructive interpersonal relations. Teachers who subscribe to affiliative values deal with their learners in a friendly and pleasant way. They are open and sensitive to the emotional needs of their learners.

Affiliative values are related to the professional ethics that underlie teaching practices in the classroom. *Ethics* are common sense moral rules, such as:

- Avoid harming others.
- Respect the right of others.
- Do not lie or cheat.
- Keep promises.
- Obey the law.
- Prevent harm to others.
- Help those in need.
- Be fair.

In teaching ethical issues are concerned with how teachers perform their helping relationship with learners. Inherent to any helping relationship is the potential for misconduct and learner abuse. Teachers can let personal values stand in the way of good education practice; they can use the power inherent in their professional role to abuse learners (even if unintentionally). Ethics is about doing the right thing. It is about how teachers should behave towards their learners in the classroom. How teachers treat their learners generally demonstrates their personal system of values.

Successful teachers honour and strive to model the following *ten* affiliative values:[2]

1. self-respect;
2. personal growth;
3. responsibility;
4. social rights;
5. purposeful living;
6. self-discipline;
7. personal integrity;
8. fairness/justice;
9. self-acceptance; and
10. forgiveness.

We can make a difference simply by choosing to do so. We can start our day by saying, "I choose to make a difference today," and see where that attitude takes us. (Marie Russell)

---

[2] See Glossary of terms on page 141 for an explanation of these values.

Emotional Intelligence in the Classroom

> **! Try this now!**
>
> Complete the *Teacher personal values clarification inventory*[TM3] to gain a deeper understanding of your personal values.

Teacher personal values clarification inventory[TM3]

Rate each question below on a scale of 1 to 5, according to how true it is for you.

1	2	3	4	5
Not important at all				Extremely important

1. I have the right to honour my needs and wants, to treat them as important. The same applies to those I interact with daily. ____
2. I deserve to be treated courteously and with respect by everyone. Others deserve to be treated courteously and with respect by me. ____
3. I am worthy of happiness and so are other people.
4. No one has the right to force ideas and values on me that I do not accept. I do not have the right to force my ideas and values on others. ____
5. I deserve to succeed at what I attempt and so do other people. ____
6. Self-development and self-fulfillment are appropriate moral goals. ____
7. To remain effective, I need to keep expanding my knowledge: continuous learning is a way of life. ____
8. The better I know and understand myself, the better the life I can create. ____
9. I am better served by correcting my mistakes than by pretending they do not exist. ____
10. Mistakes are not grounds for self-condemnation. ____
11. I am responsible for my choices and actions. Other people are responsible for theirs. ____
12. I am responsible for my behaviour towards other people. ____
13. I am responsible for the quality of my communication. ____
14. I am responsible for my personal happiness. ____
15. I have the right to express myself in appropriate ways in appropriate contexts. ____
16. I have the right to stand up for my convictions. Other people have the right to stand up for theirs. ____
17. I have the right to treat my values and feelings as important. Other people have the right to treat their values and feelings as important too. ____
18. If I am to succeed, I need to learn how to achieve my goals and purposes. I need to develop and then implement a plan of action. ____

---

[3] Developed by the authors.

19. If I am to succeed, I need to pay attention to the outcome of my actions. ____
20. It is important to practise self-discipline not as a sacrifice but as a natural precondition for being able to achieve my desires. ____
21. It is important to practise what I preach. ____
22. It is important to keep my promises and honour my commitments. ____
23. I do not share personal information that I know about others and/or that has been entrusted to me confidentially, regardless of how I gained it. I honour the right of others to privacy. ____
24. I keep clear boundaries between my personal and professional life. ____
25. It is important to strive to make my life a reflection of my inner vision of the good. ____
26. It is important to deal with other human beings fairly, justly, benevolently, and compassionately. ____
27. It is important to strive for moral consistency. ____
28. I accept that what I think, feel or do is an expression of myself in the moment it occurs: I am not bound by thoughts, feelings or actions that I cannot sanction; but neither do I evade their reality or pretend they are not mine. ____
29. I accept the reality of my problems, but I am not defined by them. My fear, pain, confusion or mistakes are not my essence. ____
30. I forgive myself and others for perceived mistakes or errors in judgement. By accepting myself and others unconditionally and allowing myself to let all guilt and resentment go, I free myself and others to make better choices. ____

Self-respect	**Self-discipline**
1. ____	20 ____
2. ____	Sub-total: ____ (+4) = ____
3. ____	
4. ____	
5. ____	
Sub-total: ____	
Personal growth	**Personal integrity**
6. ____	21. ____
7. ____	22. ____
8. ____	23. ____
9. ____	24. ____
10. ____	25. ____
Sub-total: ____	Sub-total: ____

Responsibility 11. _____ 12. _____ 13. _____ 14. _____ Sub-total: _____ (+1) = _____	**Fairness/justice** 26. _____ 27. _____ Sub-total: _____ (+3) = _____
Social rights 15. _____ 16. _____ 17. _____ Sub-total: _____ (+ 2) = _____	**Self-acceptance** 28. _____ 29. _____ Sub-total: _____ (+3) = _____
Purposeful living 18. _____ 19. _____ Sub-total: _____ (+3) = _____	**Forgiveness** 30. _____ Sub-total: _____ (+4) = _____

Transfer your total score for each of the ten values to the chart below.

Value	Score	Value	Score
Self-respect	_____	Personal growth	_____
Responsibility	_____	Social rights	_____
Purposeful living	_____	Self-discipline	_____
Personal integrity	_____	Fairness/justice	_____
Self-acceptance	_____	Forgiveness	_____

The higher your overall score for a particular value, the more important that value is to you. On the lines provided, rank in order each value according to the score you have accumulated. The resulting list gives you insight into how you treat your learners and the emotional climate evident in your classroom as a result of your value preferences.

For an emotional climate that fosters optimal learning and teaching you may need to consider the importance of all the values on the checklist provided.

! Try this now!

Review your value preferences and the factors that influence the emotional climate in the classroom. Think about the classroom atmosphere that you deal with daily. Write a personal value statement to indicate your willingness to improve and/or create a classroom atmosphere that fosters optimal learning and growth. See table 3.2 for an example of a personal values statement.

Table 3.2 Statement of personal values

Value preferences
The learners have the right to know – at any time – my objectives and rationale for whatever I am doing.
Learners always have the choice of participating or not participating in any class group activity that I offer.
I assume that learners are unique and learn in different ways and at different rates.
I consider conflict and resistance to be a natural outgrowth of the differences and interactions between people; I do not consider them to be negative or destructive. Although conflict and resistance may not be resolved, they can be managed.
I see my role as educator to include protecting learners from personal embarrassment, scapegoating or behaviours that I feel may be personally destructive to them and to the classroom environment.

The power of words

> John is a learner who suffers severe rejection at home. He finds it difficult to concentrate on his schoolwork and tends to isolate himself in class. Mrs Ngokha is an excellent mathematics teacher. She feels very frustrated and tense because John is not concentrating. When she asks him a question, he merely stares back in blank surprise. This makes her lose her temper. She shouts at him: "John, you idiot! I hate learners like you! What are you doing in my classroom anyway? I don't need failures like you." John meekly whispers, "I'm sorry, Miss. You're right."

How teachers communicate with learners in the classroom has a huge influence on their sense of psychological safety, their self-image, their feeling of belonging and their sense of competence. Being authority figures, teachers have the power to either build or damage the self-esteem of children. Apart from imparting knowledge, communication in the classroom revolves mostly around sending messages out about the learners' abilities and innate capacities regarding how they master the tasks at hand.

Teachers who do not recognise the power of their words can unintentionally demean learners. Being very vulnerable, learners internalise both positive and negative messages and information about themselves. Unfortunately, it is the more negative messages that make a lasting impression. By absorbing these negative messages the self-esteem of learners is lowered. This leads to withdrawal behaviour and poor performance.

When teachers are not sensitive about the unconscious messages that learners send through their behaviour, they unintentionally worsen the learners' negative emotional state by their choice of words and their body language. Successful teachers understand why it is important to develop their communication skills as part of their repertoire of emotional intelligence.

Teachers who are good communicators are sensitive towards the vulnerability and emotional state of their learners. They carefully choose what they say and how they communicate. Often the teacher's tone of voice is influenced by learners' inattentiveness or restlessness. However, because they are able to read the learners' mood and non-verbal behavioural cues, emotionally intelligent teachers adjust their tone of voice, body language and general behaviour when addressing learners. They understand the magic of radiating enthusiasm and patience. They use humour to create a friendly, relaxed atmosphere in the classroom.

Laughter that is not cruel or destructive is healthy and healing. It can encourage learners to open up to teachers. A patient, kind and understanding tone of voice helps learners to find the courage and confidence to respond in more truthful ways to the teacher.

Poor communicators are not sufficiently aware of their learners' emotional needs and communicate in inappropriate ways. They are not aware of their listeners while speaking. They fail to respond to the verbal and non-verbal feedback which tells them how the interaction is going. Our body language is like a telegraph for our thoughts, attitudes, feelings and intentions.

Table 3.3 Reading body language

Messages	Meaning
Eyes looking down or away	Self-consciousness or guilt
Raised eyebrow	Disbelief
Rubbing the nose or pulling the ears	They do not understand, even if they say they do
Smiling when greeting someone	Friendly intentions, positive attitude
Hand touching the mouth	Anxious or trying to deceive someone
Folded or crossed arms	Nervous or shut off from someone (or feeling cold)
Hands on hips or active gesturing	Aggression
Tapping on the desk or chair	Nervousness or impatience
Tremor in voice	Nervousness
Shrugging the shoulders	Indifference to what someone says
Facing you squarely, full height, smiling, head forward	Confidence

> **! Try this now!**
>
> **How do you come across?**
>
> There is a special technique that uses a video camera monitor to explore the effect you make on your learners, particularly in relation to non-verbal communication. You need another person to help you with this.
>
> - Sit in a chair facing the video monitor, while your assistant focuses the video camera on you.
> - Let the camera operator invite you to talk about yourself for about four minutes. The focus of the camera should be slowly changed to include close-ups, long shots and shots that concentrate on particular areas of your face and body.
> - While you look at yourself on the monitor, have the other person gently ask the following questions:
>
>   "Does this person draw your attention?"
>
>   "Do you dislike what you hear?"
>
>   "What are your feelings towards him or her?"
>
>   Then think about what helps or hinders your message.
> - Is your body language congruent with your message or does it distract from it?
> - How could you improve your presentation?
> - At the end of the exercise, replay the whole video and explore your feelings after the tape has been seen.

Remember, body language is not universal – different cultures have their own gestures and ignorance can inadvertently result in offence. Emotionally intelligent teachers are sensitive to how they come across to learners. When we communicate we rely more on the message contained in the body language of the communicator than what is actually said. Our body, including posture, gesture and facial expression, even our physical appearance (the way we dress) constantly sends messages to others (including our learners) and makes powerful statements about who we are, how we feel and what we think.

Learners feel accepted or rejected according to what they read in the body language of the teacher. The teacher's body language and tone of voice can determine the general classroom atmosphere. Teachers who smile and greet learners in a friendly voice make them feel respected and welcome in the classroom. Teachers who are moody and grumpy make learners feel rejected and negatively influence their ability to concentrate on learning tasks. Table 3.4 contrasts dysfunctional teacher responses with emotionally intelligent teacher responses to classroom behaviour.

Table 3.4 Dysfunctional responses vs emotionally intelligent responses to classroom behaviour

Dysfunctional behaviours	Emotionally intelligent behaviours
Alienating - Continually stresses conformity - Fails to encourage - Fails to give verbal responses - Listens passively, rather than actively	**Empathic** - Builds rapport - Identifies feelings - Sensitive to emotional needs
Critical - Points out inconsistencies - Repeatedly mentions weaknesses - Belittles	**Supportive** - Acknowledges problems, concerns, feelings - Accepts differences of opinion - Shows understanding - Communicates availability - Commits to support - Expresses trust
Directive - Prescribes - Gives orders - Threatens - Fails to provide options - Quotes rules and regulations - Points out only one acceptable way	**Exploring** - Asks open-ended questions - Reflects - Shares - Probes
Language patterns - "I am going to make mincemeat of you if you don't listen to me!" - "You'd better listen to me or I'll kick you out of my class!" - "I'm the boss in this class. If you are not interested in this work, you don't need to attend this class, anyway … I just want to finish this lesson." - "… so don't even think of asking questions … don't waste my time!" - "Don't expect me to remember your names … I have a lot of work to cover." - "Don't even try to think you are special … there are too many children in this class." - "Don't try to act smart with me … I don't have time for smart guys."	**Language patterns** - "How are you all feeling today?" - "I really appreciate the effort you've made." - "I'm confident we can achieve these goals." - "What do you think …?" - "You sure have done a good job, thank you!" - "I am really pleased with what we have accomplished." - "How can we improve our classroom?" - "I really like the idea. It will help us." - "I am really proud of you!" - "Thank you for helping me!" - "I appreciate how we all work as a team." - "Now I understand better what you have been trying to tell me."

Kindling warmth in the classroom 47

> **Taking action!**
>
> *Three suggestions to put the ideas of this chapter into practice:*
>
> 1. Assess your behavioural style in the classroom by clarifying your values. Identify those values that you need to adopt to improve the emotional climate in the classroom. Clarify your values by reviewing your personal values statement. Knowing your values may help you gain insight into how you treat your learners.
> 2. Study the factors that constitute the classroom climate. Identify actions or steps you can take to address the emotional needs of your learners.
> 3. Assess on a daily basis the emotional climate in your classroom. Is it a predominant cold or a predominantly warm atmosphere? How did your mood or emotional-mental state influence your behaviour? Did your values play a role in helping you to manage your emotions?

Review questions

1. Describe the characteristics of a high nurturance, warm classroom atmosphere.
2. How do the values and professional ethics of teachers influence the classroom atmosphere?
3. Why is it important for teachers to take cognizance of the classroom climate?
4. Explain the factors that influence the classroom climate.
5. What can teachers do to create psychological safety in the classroom? Why are the physical conditions of the classroom also important?
6. Explain what teachers can do to create a positive self-image and feelings of belonging in the classroom.
7. Why must teachers be good communicators?
8. Explain how the physical appearance, body language, general demeanour and behavioural style of the teacher influence the learning and motivation of learners.
9. How does an emotionally warm classroom climate differ from a cold classroom atmosphere? What are the typical language patterns and style characteristics of the teacher in each case?
10. What are your key values? How do your values influence the way you feel about and treat people?

✓ In a snapshot

1. The classroom environment refers to the conditions, circumstances and influences surrounding and affecting the development and performance of learners. These include, for example, the physical conditions of the school and classroom, the teacher's physical appearance, body language, behaviour and attitudes towards learners.

2. To a large extent the personal values of teachers influence how they treat and interact with their learners.

3. The classroom climate is the shared perception of learners about the classroom environment, that is, how they think and feel they are being treated by the teacher. The classroom climate can range from a warm, welcoming and nurturing atmosphere to one that is characterised by coldness and indifference as evident in the behaviour of the teacher.

4. Effective teachers are knowledgeable of and competent in establishing the factors that establish a high nurturance, emotionally warm classroom climate.

5. How teachers communicate with their learners has a profound impact on their sense of psychological safety, self-image, feelings of belonging and sense of personal competence.

6. Effective teachers are aware of how their language patterns and non-verbal communication with learners influence their mental-emotional state.

Suggested reading

Barth, JM., Dunlap, ST., Dane, H., Lochman, JE. & Well, KC. (2004) 'Classroom environment influences on aggression, peer relations, and academic focus' *Journal of School Psychology*, 42: 115–133

Morris, E. (2002) 'Emotional literacy training for educators: Developing the whole person – linking hearts and minds in all learners' *Gifted Education International*, 16: 133–137

Salovey, P. & Mayer, JD. (1990) 'Emotional intelligence' *Imagination, Cognition, and Personality*, 9: 185–211

Sterret, EA. (2000) *The Manager's Pocket Guide to Emotional Intelligence*. Amherst, MA: HRD Press

Tolle, E. (2001) *Practising the Power of Now*. London: Hodder & Stoughton

Walsch, ND. (2005) *What God Wants: A Compelling Answer to Humanity's Biggest Question*. London: Hodder Mobius

Chapter 4: The power of managing emotions

In chapter 3 we explored the factors that determine the classroom climate. This chapter offers practical suggestions for developing or expanding emotional intelligence that establish and foster an emotionally warm classroom climate. Emotional intelligence is an intelligence which successful people bring to their working lives and to their social interaction with others.

Emily Sterrett (2000) writes that true emotional intelligence is the ability to call upon information from the emotional centre of the brain (see chapter 2) and to balance that with information from the rational centre of the brain. Based on a number of recent studies, experts now believe that IQ, or general intelligence, contributes no more than 25% to one's overall success in life. Case studies and longitudinal studies by highly regarded researchers indicate that while opportunity or serendipity could add a few percentage points, many well-respected people create their own opportunities. They succeed because they rank high on all dimensions of emotional intelligence.

People are about as happy as they make up their minds to be. (Abraham Lincoln)

Tsepo was a teacher who prided himself on his discipline and fairness towards his learners. It was true: Tsepo's learners nearly always used the word "assertive" and "fair" to describe him. However, they used other words too: "unapproachable" and "cold". When Tsepo's closest cousin was dying of HIV/AIDS, he did not share this news with anyone at school. He put on a stoic face and tried to concentrate on his teaching. His colleagues and learners speculated about what might be wrong, because Tsepo seemed more edgy than usual. He was also out of the classroom a lot. No one learned about the situation until after his cousin's death. Said one colleague, "He would be a lot more human if he'd just let his hair down a little bit."

What do we mean by emotional intelligence?

> *When strong emotions occur it is essential first to pay attention to them. Take time to work with your emotions; don't ignore them ... more needs to be done in the way of giving yourself space and time to experience what is happening. This may mean getting away from what you are doing, taking an hour or so away from work, going for long walks. Don't ignore your feelings or pretend they don't exist. Above all, don't ignore your emotions because you are fearful of them.*
> *(Dona Witten)*

Emotional intelligence is based on having a positive self-attitude and enough self-knowledge to recognise our feelings about ourselves, others and the life situations we deal with daily. It is about recognising the impact of our emotional state on ourselves and those we interact with and the skills to make the right decision regarding an emotion.

The thinking brain makes decisions about emotions. However, not all emotions need to be expressed. They also do not need to be hidden or denied. Emily Sterrett (2000) writes that emotionally intelligent people display feelings that are relevant. They deal positively with those emotions that they do not show. Such people show self-control at an appropriate or balanced level. They are consistently judged by others as less impatient, more willing to share ideas and more willing listen to the ideas of others. They are less likely to be involved in conflict and are generally more likeable. When we have the right amount of self-control, we also manage our moods well.

Chapter 2 showed how self-control helps us to recognise our feelings and emotions, to reason intelligently about our emotions and to use our awareness of our emotional state to consciously behave in a socially responsible manner. In other words, we consciously choose to behave in a way that does not only promote our own health and well-being but that creates healthy and positive connections with the people around us.

We learned that emotions are energy in motion. Our emotions are the primary motivating forces that arouse, direct and sustain activity. Emotional intelligence describes the extent to which we are able to tap into our feelings and emotions as a source of energy to guide our thinking and actions. Emotional intelligence involves our ability to manage our emotional life cognitively with greater or lesser skill.

This skill entails a unique set of competencies, such as emotional self-awareness, assertiveness, self-regard, empathy, interpersonal relations, social responsibility, problem-solving, flexibility, stress tolerance, happiness and optimism.

Emotional self-awareness, assertiveness, the ability to empathise with others and the ability to adjust our feelings, thoughts, and behaviour to changing circumstances and situations (in other words flexibility) are the essence of emotional intelligence. These competencies enable us to be more efficient in problem-solving and interpersonal relationships. Overall they help us to feel content and satisfied with ourselves and others. They enable us to enjoy life and to feel happy.

All of these competencies are dependent upon a positive self-regard, the ability to be assertive and to behave in a socially responsible manner towards ourselves and others. In addition, optimism and the ability to tolerate stressful situations help us to be effective in problem-solving. Let's take a closer look at these emotional competencies.

Emotional competencies

Reuven Bar-On (1997) describes emotional competencies as follows:

Emotional self-awareness makes people consciously aware of their emotions. These people are said to be in touch with their feelings and emotions. They know exactly what they are feeling and they understand why they feel the way they do.

Assertiveness enables people to openly express their feelings, thoughts and beliefs and to defend their rights in a non-destructive manner. These people are not over-controlling or shy. They express their feelings (outwardly and often directly), without being aggressive or abusive.

Self-regard generally gives people good feelings about themselves. They tend to accept and respect themselves. Essentially they like the way they are. They are sure of themselves because they know who they are. They accept their strengths and weaknesses and are aware of both their limitations and possibilities.

Empathy generally makes people aware of and appreciative of the feelings of others. Empathetic people are sensitive towards the feelings of others. They can tune in to what, how and why people feel the way they do. Being empathetic means being able to emotionally read other people. Empathetic people care about others and show interest in and concern for them.

Interpersonal relations enable people to establish and maintain mutually satisfying relationships that are generally characterised by the capacity for intimacy and the ability to give and receive affection. They desire to cultivate friendly relations with others, feel at ease and comfortable in such relations and possess positive expectations concerning their social interaction.

Social responsibility enables people to act in a responsible manner, even though they may not benefit personally. Such people have a social consciousness and a basic concern for the well-being of others. They generally have positive feelings towards others. They have the ability to do things for and with others, to accept others, to act in accordance with their conscience and to uphold social rules.

Problem-solving helps people to be conscientious, disciplined, methodical and systematic. People who are good at problem-solving persevere in their approach to problems. They desire to do their best and confront, rather than avoid problems.

Flexibility enables people to adjust their emotions, feelings, thoughts and behaviours according to changing situations and conditions. These people are able to adapt to unfamiliar, unpredictable and dynamic circumstances. They are agile and capable of responding to change. Generally they are open to and tolerant of different ideas, orientations, ways and practices.

Stress tolerance makes people able to withstand adverse events and stressful situations, without falling apart. Such people are generally calm and rarely get overly anxious or agitated. They are resourceful and effective in dealing with difficult situations. They are optimistic about new experiences and change in general because they believe that they can face and handle these situations.

Happiness is associated with a general feeling of cheerfulness and enthusiasm. Happy people feel satisfied with their lives and generally derive pleasure from life. They have a happy disposition and are pleasant to be with. They are able to let their hair down and enjoy opportunities for having fun.

Optimism assumes a measure of hope in one's approach to life. It is a positive approach to daily living. Optimistic people look at the brighter side of life and maintain a positive attitude, even in the face of adversity.

Although emotional intelligence develops over a lifespan and can be enhanced through training, it is important to note that we are not always aware of why we are doing something, or what we are doing. This is because our unconscious reactions to outside events and people are influenced by our feelings, beliefs and thoughts about ourselves, that is, by our self-esteem or self-regard. From this perspective many emotions defy our conscious control and regulation.

We spend so much of our lives worrying and trying to prevent the bad from happening in our lives that we forget to enjoy the good! What a waste of a life! (Susan Jeffers)

Self-esteem makes the difference

Chapter 1 explained that how we feel about ourselves affects the quality of our relationship with others. If we feel bad about ourselves, it will be more difficult for us to reach out to others. At the same time, it becomes much more difficult to allow other people into our lives.

Our thoughts, beliefs and feelings about ourselves influence what we project about ourselves. This is also tacitly picked up by others. If we feel that we are not interesting or worthy, other people (including our learners) will sense this. They will find it hard to regard us as interesting or worthy, even if they think so.

John Mulligan (1988) writes that if we feel we are not worth caring for or not worth loving, it becomes difficult for others to communicate to us that they do care for us. It becomes difficult for us to take their feelings seriously. If we struggle to have honest relationships with others, it is most probably because we feel badly about ourselves. We may be too worried about what others think of us. We may find that our feelings are easily hurt, and that we take offence at other people's comments (particularly our learners).

When we feel good about ourselves, we are more relaxed when interacting with others. We feel less concerned about what others (including our learners) might be thinking or saying. People generally listen to us and take us seriously. When we respect ourselves, others do too. Developing emotional intelligence increases self-esteem because our self-confidence in connecting with others in healthier ways grows increasingly.

You will only begin to change your life when you learn how to love yourself properly. (Louise Hay)

Emotional intelligence can be broken down into three behavioural dimensions or areas: the cognitive dimension, the affective dimension and the social dimension.

Behavioural profile of the emotionally intelligent teacher

Cognitive dimension

The cognitive aspect of emotional intelligence refers to how we think and reason about our feelings and emotions. It relates to intelligent reasoning about the emotions we experience. Our research in the school environment indicates that emotionally intelligent teachers preserve their composure when exerting classroom discipline.

They are assertive and maintain discipline in a gentle but firm manner. They express their feelings outwardly without being aggressive or abusive towards their learners.

Emotionally intelligent teachers are rarely unsettled by uncomfortable feelings of self-consciousness or bashfulness. They tend to be in touch with their feelings and emotions, have a high self-regard and self-awareness.

Our research further indicates that teachers who are not able to display emotionally intelligent behaviour towards their learners come across as being authoritarian and harsh. For example, such teachers shout at learners, chase them out of the classroom and mete out arbitrary corporal punishment. They could even engage in abuse such as kicking learners' shins or instructing them to attend detention classes as a solution to misbehaviour. For example, one teacher instructed learners to sit in the shade of a tree and not on the stoep on a day when the temperature was 30° Celsius. Learners experience these teachers as being unreasonable, unfair, extremely disrespectful and non-caring about their welfare. Another example is of the teacher who would not allow the team to drink water on a very hot day and who chased learners away from the team when they drank water.

Affective dimension

The affective aspect of emotional intelligence deals with how we feel, including our mood and emotional state, and how we use our emotions to be creative about our lives and interactions. It is about living from our hearts and entails the ability to harness our emotions and moods as a source of energy to positively influence our well-being, personal goals and plans, and our performance as educators.

The affective dimension includes the ability to honestly assess how self-regard influences our mood and general emotional state. Adult behaviour is generally regarded as a reflection of one's personal feelings about oneself.

Our research indicates that a happy disposition (evident in the passion and enthusiasm demonstrated by the teacher for the subject he or she teaches) can motivate learners to perform well in the subject.

A happy disposition is generally associated with a feeling of cheerfulness and enthusiasm. Happiness is a barometric indicator for our overall degree of emotional intelligence and emotional functioning. People who are able to look at the brighter side of life have a positive approach to daily living. They are able to maintain a positive attitude, even in the face of adversity.

> *Here is what learners had to say:*
>
> *Passion and enthusiasm*
>
> - *I cannot believe that there are some teachers who appear to hate children. They can be very impatient and irritable with us children. I believe a teacher must have a real passion for children. Isn't that the reason why you chose to become a teacher?*
> - *For me the ideal teacher must also have a passion for his or her subject. I had such a teacher in Grade 6. The teacher made the subject so interesting and lively that I always gave of my best for that subject. I never wanted to disappoint that teacher, never!*

Social dimension

This aspect of emotinal intelligence deals with how we respond to and interact with others as a result of the cognitive and affective aspects. It is about how we balance the rational and emotional brain to achieve inner harmony and well-being: the secret of feeling happy.

The social aspect of emotionally intelligent behaviour is about our personal effectiveness in interpersonal relations. It includes the ability to notice and make distinctions between other people's moods, temperaments, motivations and intentions. It is the ability to use this information to regulate and guide our thinking and actions in a socially acceptable manner.

Our research indicates that emotionally intelligent teachers have an emotionally warm style by showing empathy towards their learners. People who are able to show empathy to others are generally aware of and can appreciate the feelings of others. They are sensitive to others' feelings and are able to emotionally read other people. They tend to care about others and show interest in and concern for others.

A warm emotional style establishes and maintains mutually satisfying relationships. The ability to do this is an emotional skill which requires sensitivity towards others and a desire to establish meaningful relations that are potentially rewarding and enjoyable.

Emotionally intelligent teachers have a positive attitude towards their learners and treat them with respect. They make learners feel honoured for their uniqueness by allowing them to openly express their feelings, beliefs and thoughts.

A loving relationship can provide nourishment in all areas of life. It can generate energy enough, not only for itself, but also for work, family, friends, hobbies. But this doesn't happen by magic. A relationship is like a garden. If it is not watered, weeded, pruned, fertilised — cared for — its yield suffers.
(Charles and Caroline Muir)

Here is what learners had to say:

Providing guidance and emotional support

- My teacher helps me to achieve success even when I struggle. She always supports and guides me. I know she is there for me.
- She will search for help or advice from others to guide and assist me. I will never forget her. What a special person she is!

Accepting learners unconditionally for their uniqueness

- My teacher doesn't compare me with other children. I am a person in my own right.
- I am accepted for who I am. I am allowed to express my own opinion.
- She looks me directly in the eye. I can truly trust her because she really listens.

Treating learners with respect

- My teacher speaks in a respectful tone when addressing me. I know she respects me and it makes me feel special.
- My teacher calls us by our names and will not humiliate us in front of our classmates.
- She treats me with respect ... like a person.

Empathy

- My teacher really cares about our needs. I have never heard her saying bad things about us to other children. I just love studying her subject!

Emotionally intelligent teachers act in a socially responsible manner towards learners. They are willing to provide guidance and support until learners are able to master their assignments and classroom tasks. For example, they do not mind to explain repeatedly what is expected regarding the homework or assignments.

People with a positive self-esteem are able to show caring and compassion for others. They are concerned about their well-being, growth and development. Their experience of self-worth derives from being authentic. They tend to act in a socially responsible manner towards their learners. Our research indicates that socially responsible behaviour in a teacher greatly assists in creating an emotionally warm classroom atmosphere where learners feel secure and safe. Emotionally intelligent teachers make a concerted effort to include all learners in a team. They motivate all learners to perform to the best of their ability.

Impact of the teacher's behaviour on the classroom climate

Generally, our research indicates that teachers who demonstrate emotionally intelligent behaviour are able to create an emotionally warm classroom climate which generates positive emotions within both teacher and learner. Asserting discipline in ways that preserve self-respect seems to contribute towards an experience of emotional security. The findings suggest that by honouring the uniqueness of learners and creating a climate of acceptance and caring, learners generally feel empowered to build a positive self-image of who they are and what they are capable of. Chapter 3 showed how the feeling of belonging and emotional security reduces learners' feelings of isolation. In fact, it appears to facilitate feelings of pride in their own and their group's achievements.

Research has demonstrated that the ability to manage emotions contributes positively to the quality of social interaction. People who are socially well-adapted tend to display emotionally intelligent behaviour. They tend to be aware of their own emotions and how they impact on others with their overt behaviour. They are able to express their emotions in more appropriate ways. They are better able to read and respond to the emotions of others in social interactions. Figure 4.1 illustrates how emotionally intelligent teachers use their emotional and cognitive presence to monitor the socio-emotional climate in the classroom and to engage in behaviour that facilitates emotional security within themselves and their learners.

Self-awareness and intelligent reasoning about one's emotions allow for adaptive responses and a problem-solving approach. Constant navigation of one's cognitive and affective self-presentation affects the emotional climate in the classroom. Emotionally intelligent behaviour leads to rapport between teachers and learners which in turn creates a sense of security, identity, belonging, purpose and competence (as discussed in chapter 3).

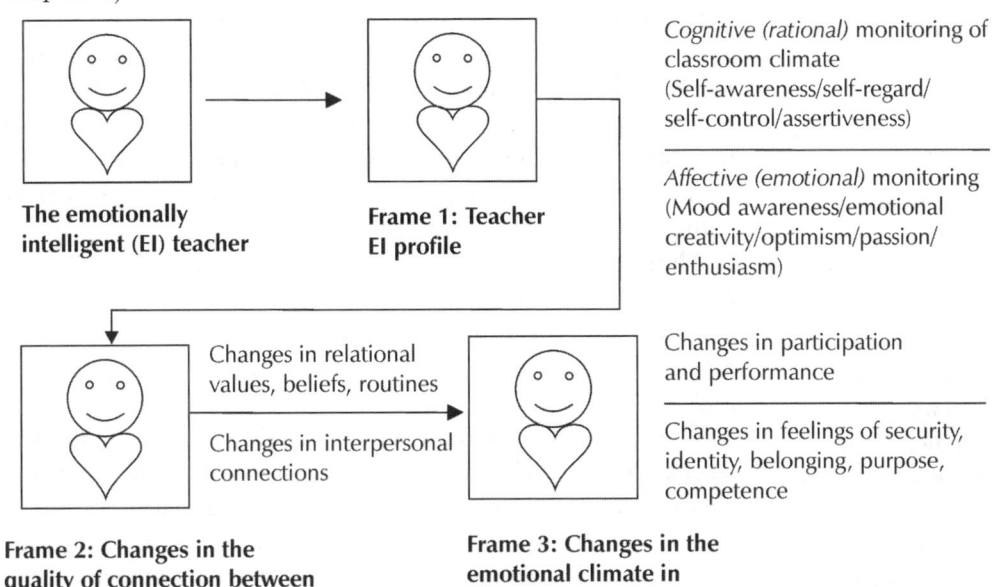

The emotionally intelligent (EI) teacher

Frame 1: Teacher EI profile

Cognitive (rational) monitoring of classroom climate (Self-awareness/self-regard/self-control/assertiveness)

Affective (emotional) monitoring (Mood awareness/emotional creativity/optimism/passion/enthusiasm)

Changes in relational values, beliefs, routines

Changes in interpersonal connections

Changes in participation and performance

Changes in feelings of security, identity, belonging, purpose, competence

Frame 2: Changes in the quality of connection between teacher and learners

Frame 3: Changes in the emotional climate in the classroom

Figure 4.1 Impact of the teacher's behaviour on the classroom climate

Chapter 2 showed how the emotional states of both teachers and learners have an important effect on attention, focus, perception and time spent on tasks, ultimately on the learners' performance in the classroom. Teachers who demonstrate emotionally intelligent behaviour in the classroom are more effective in achieving the academic goals they have set. Emotionally intelligent teachers convey a sense of caring for their learners and create an emotional climate that enhances the learning environment, reduces peer conflict and creates a more desirable teaching situation.

How often do you tell the special people in your life exactly what it is that you love most about them?

Although you are unique, you have probably noticed that you have some behaviours in common with other people. Conversely, some people have behaviours that are different to yours. Each one of us has a particular way of approaching life (including, of course, our emotional life). There are certain patterns that exist in our behaviour. Other people with patterns similar to ours share our preferences, particularly the way we make decisions, solve problems and relate to other people (and thus treat our learners).

Understanding ourselves

Learning more about our primary way of relating to the world around us can lead to understanding ourselves and others better. We will know why it is that at times we find it easy to behave in an emotionally intelligent way and why in other instances we struggle to display emotionally intelligent behaviour when interacting with others.

We either have a *thinking* or a *feeling* preference in the way we make decisions, solve problems, communicate and interact. Both thinking and feeling are rational ways of making decisions and reaching conclusions. For example, thinking types prefer to relate to the world and other people, such as our learners, from a logical and objective or a subjective values-based standpoint.

Thinking types prefer the use of logic and rationality as the basis for problem-solving, without the feelings of others entering into the process. While they have and use values and emotions to decide, these are used only to support their logical conclusions.

The strengths of thinking types include working out what is wrong with something so that they can apply their problem-solving. They try to remove themselves mentally from a situation to examine it objectively and analyse the cause and effect. Thinking types come across as tough-minded, impersonal, critical and task-driven.

Feeling types prefer to have social harmony around them. They get along with others and are sympathetic. They mentally place themselves within a situation and identify with the people involved. This enables them to make decisions based on person-centred values. Their goal is harmony and recognition of individuals.

The strengths of feeling types include understanding, appreciating and supporting others. People see them as sympathetic, tender-hearted, compassionate and accepting. While feeling types use logic and reason to decide, these are used only to support their values-oriented conclusions.

Although we all use our thinking (impersonal logic and rationality) and feeling (person-centred values-based logic and rationality) mental functions when making decisions and solving problems, we will have one of the two functions as a strength and the other as a weak, or undifferentiated function. We will prefer to use one function and may tend to neglect the other function.

> *All human beings have the potential to be their best self. All of us have the seeds of grace, compassion, wisdom, and love within us. Whatever we expect to occur in life, tends to become what we encounter; so when you choose to notice and respond to the nobility in those around you, there is a much greater likelihood that is what you will find in them.*
> (Denise Linn)

The power of managing emotions

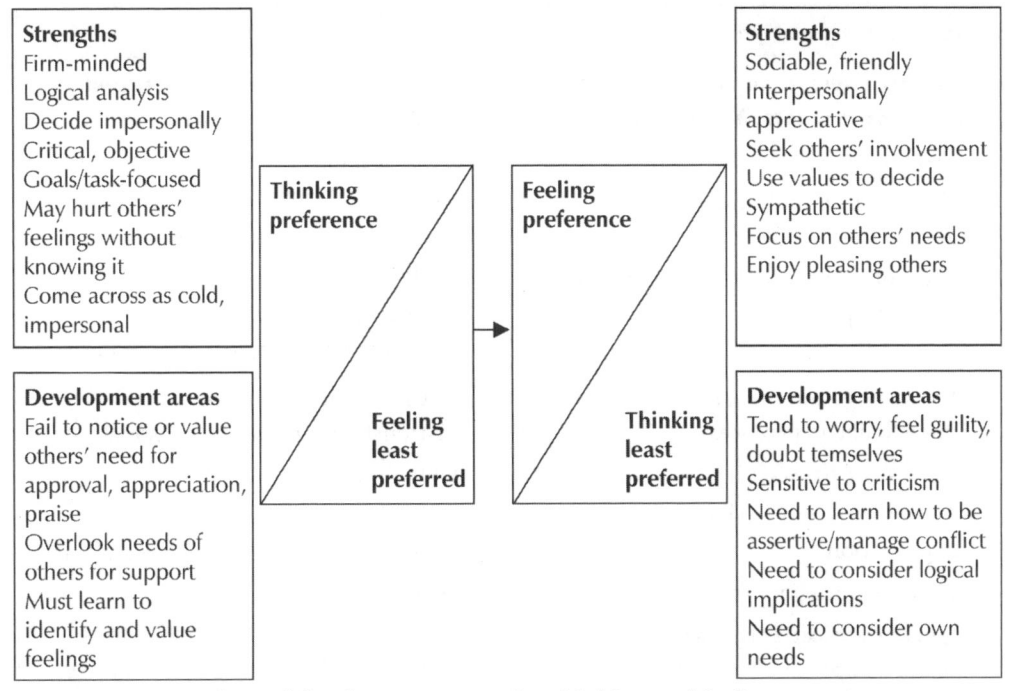

Strengths Firm-minded Logical analysis Decide impersonally Critical, objective Goals/task-focused May hurt others' feelings without knowing it Come across as cold, impersonal	**Strengths** Sociable, friendly Interpersonally appreciative Seek others' involvement Use values to decide Sympathetic Focus on others' needs Enjoy pleasing others
Thinking preference → **Feeling preference**	
Feeling least preferred / **Thinking least preferred**	
Development areas Fail to notice or value others' need for approval, appreciation, praise Overlook needs of others for support Must learn to identify and value feelings	**Development areas** Tend to worry, feel guilty, doubt themselves Sensitive to criticism Need to learn how to be assertive/manage conflict Need to consider logical implications Need to consider own needs

Figure 4.2 Strengths and development areas for thinking and feeling types

Weak decision-making, problem-solving and communication with others can often be traced back to not using the less preferred function. This imbalanced use of the two mental functions creates many of the imbalances in our interpersonal communication with other people and how we treat our learners in the classroom.

> **! Try this now!**
>
> **What is your preference?**
>
> Thinking and feeling preferences are revealed in the way we communicate with other people and how we decide. They apply to the way we behave in relationships.
>
> **Thinking types** focus their communication on data and things that are based on principles. They relate to others in a more impersonal and objective way and are interested in communicating about personal matters.
>
> **Feeling types** relate to others in a more personal and emotional way. They focus their communication on people issues and the values that are important to them. They are less interested in impersonal discussions of data and things.
>
> As you read through the following statements, choose the preference that best matches your communication style and relationship behaviour.
>
> Once you have determined your primary preference, reflect on how your preference influences the way you tend to treat or interact with your learners.
>
> *(Based on Hirsh and Kummerow, 1989)*

Communication style	
I am more likely to communicate and relate to others as a Thinker because I:	*I am more likely to communicate and relate to others as a Feeler because I:*
__ Prefer brief and concise communication.	__ Prefer sociable, friendly, and even time-consuming communication.
__ Note the pros and cons of each alternative.	__ Note how a given alternative has value and how it affects people.
__ Show objectivity and readily critique ideas and people.	__ Show appreciation and readily empathise with people and their ideas.
__ Focus my communication on tasks and impersonal occurrences.	__ Focus my communication on relationships, people and personal happenings.
__ See others' flaws.	__ See others' positive points.
__ Control my expression of kindness, love, appreciation.	__ Offer my expressions of kindness, love and appreciation.
__ Show my caring more impersonally.	__ Show my caring through personalised words and actions.
__ Ignore the niceties that are helpful in my relationships.	__ Shy away from negatives that have a potential for undermining my relationships.
__ Tolerate occasional queries as to my emotional state.	__ Appreciate frequent queries as to my emotional state.

Overusing our preferences

Both the feeling and thinking types have the potential to overuse or abuse their preferences. Naomi Quenk (1996) writes that this happens when we are under great stress or pressure. At such times, we may act in ways that are unlike our usual style because our inner harmony has been disturbed, that is, the emotional brain functions in overdrive and we are not able to interpret events and situations in our usual rational way.

It is important to recognise these experiences, as well as strategies we can use to regain inner equilibrium between the rational and emotional brains. Achieving this balance is important because it enables us to be emotionally intelligent in our social interactions. The rational brain influences the cognitive aspect of emotionally intelligent behaviour and the emotional brain influences the affective aspect of emotionally intelligent behaviour. When these two dimensions are in balance or harmony, social behaviour tends to be more emotionally intelligent.

Thinking types

Thinking types confuse the use of feeling for rational decision-making with sentimentality and emotionality. They see feeling types as overly sensitive to criticism and as needing frequent reassurance. They have trouble expressing appreciation or complimenting others verbally. They are selective in the areas that they choose to invest their feelings in. They are intensely passionate about very few things only. When one of their cherished values is disregarded, ignored or unappreciated, they may lash out at others. Accusations of coldness and lack of concern for others can be a trigger for stress, as can fears of having been excessively harsh with someone. Expressions of strong emotion by others can also set the stage for emotional outbursts. When under stress there may be a loss of the ability to think logically and to take effective action. They often focus on feeling unappreciated.

To regain equilibrium thinking types need a change of scene or to engage in some solitary physical activity. Attending to their needs and comfort is helpful. They need to experience the depths of their feeling side and to talk about it to trusted people. Silent support, a non-judgemental approach and the avoidance of direct attacks on the problem at hand, are most appreciated.

Feeling types

Feeling types can be very sensitive about how other people assess their intellectual competence. While they do not doubt their abilities, they are concerned that they might not communicate their knowledge clearly. When they compare themselves to others, they sometimes feel slow to learn and lack analytical facility. Their sensitivity about their intellectual competence makes them more attuned to comments that reflect what they perceive as their inadequacy. They then start to notice and comment on the inaccuracies by being excessively critical of other people's behaviour. When under stress, their optimism, enthusiasm and interest in people give way to withdrawal, low energy, pessimism and depression.

To regain equilibrium it helps for feeling types to experience a change of scene or listen to a friend talking about something interesting and amusing. Being outdoors or doing exercise will also help them. They also benefit from embarking on an ambitious new undertaking, even if they have to force themselves at first. They need to be taken seriously by friends and they need to be allowed to vent their feelings. Writing a journal could also help feeling types to get a handle on the problem wihout fear of external judgement or interference.

Emotional Intelligence in the Classroom

> **! Try this now!**
>
> Reflect on your preference type (thinking or feeling). Think about any stressful day you experienced at school. List the things and events that triggered those stressful responses in you. How do your responses relate to your preference type? Can you find a link? List the typical ways in which you deal with stress, particular if it triggers intense emotionalism within you.
>
> **My preference type (thinking or feeling)**
>
> **Stress triggers**
>
> **Typical things I do when I experience intense stress**
>
> **Typical things I do to deal with my stress**

Assessing emotional intelligence

The checklist that follows has been used quite successfully with educators in the school environment to improve their emotional intelligence. It is a valuable personal tool for teachers to gain an understanding of their strengths and development areas in emotional intelligence. Knowing our strengths and weaknesses can help us to chart a course for personal improvement and to reach for success in life.

> **! Try this now!**
>
> **Rate your emotional intelligence: self-assessment**
>
> The self-assessment checklist is based on the three areas of emotionally intelligent behaviour: cognitive, affective and social. It highlights those facets of emotional intelligence where you have opportunity to improve.

Self-assessment checklist

Rate each question below on a scale of 1–5, according to how true it is for you.

1	2	3	4	5
Virtually never				Virtually always

1. I am open to truly experience my feelings, both pleasant and unpleasant. ____
2. I can recognise the effect of my feelings on my body (e.g. pounding heart, fast breathing, sweating palms). ____
3. I own my feelings by accepting responsibility for feeling the way I do and take care that my feelings do not disrupt the classroom atmosphere. ____
4. I am generally comfortable in new situations. ____
5. I can investigate my emotions to find out why I respond in a certain way. ____
6. I am good at recognising my mood and I seldom bring negative emotions to the classroom. ____

The power of managing emotions 63

7. I am able to generate feelings that help me to make better choices for myself and my learners. _____
8. I neither bury my anger nor let it explode on others because I respect myself and my learners. _____
9. I let go of problems, anger or hurts from the past and I can move beyond these. _____
10. I open up appropriately to my learners, not too much, but enough so that I don't come across as cold and distant. _____
11. I can engage in healthy interactions with my learners and can size up their mood based on non-verbal signals pretty well. _____
12. My learners usually feel inspired and encouraged after talking to me.
13. I am able to sense the emotional climate of the classroom. _____
14. I am able to accurately tell my learners and others how I feel and honestly express my needs.
15. I readily admit mistakes and apologise. _____
16. I try to find the positive in any given situation and am generally optimistic about life. _____
17. I am able to put myself in my learners' shoes and see life from their point of view.
18. I can deal calmly, sensitively and proactively with the emotional displays of my learners. _____
19. I focus my full attention on my learners when I listen to them. _____
20. I usually bolster my learners' ability to grow and improve their performance. _____
21. I can listen openly to my learners without judging their opinions. _____
22. I can negotiate and resolve disagreements in the classroom. _____
23. I can motivate my learners to participate in classroom activities. _____
24. I can help my learners feel they belong in the group. _____
25. I truly respect the opinions of my learners because I value their uniqueness. _____
26. I can keep my own feelings and impulses in check, so as not to disrupt the classroom atmosphere. _____
27. I express my views honestly and thoughtfully, without being pushy. _____
28. I have a strong sense of my self-worth and capabilities. _____
29. I believe the work I do with my learners from day to day has meaning and value for them and society in general. _____
30. I take a break or use other active methods to increase energy when I sense that my energy level is getting low. _____
31. I refrain from making up my mind on issues and expressing my opinions until I have all the facts. _____

32. I feel enthusiastic about teaching my subject and can convey this to my learners. _____
33. I love being a teacher because I believe I can make a difference in the lives of my learners. _____
34. I handle classroom discipline in a firm but gentle manner because I respect myself and my learners. _____
35. I generally feel good about myself because I believe I am worthy of being loved. _____

Scoring the self-assessment checklist

1. Enter your ratings for each question in the category where it appears.
2. Add up the ratings for each category to obtain a total for that specific facet of emotional intelligence.

Cognitive behaviour	Affective behaviour	Social behaviour
How we think and reason about our feelings and emotions	How we feel, including our mood and emotional state and how we use our emotions to be creative about our lives and interactions, living from our hearts	How we respond to and interact with others as a result of the cognitive and affective aspects of our emotional intelligence, how we balance the rational and emotional brain to achieve inner harmony and well-being, the secret of feeling happy
Self-awareness 2. ___ 3. ___ 5. ___ *Self-regard* 28. ___ 35. ___ *Self-control* 8. ___ 18. ___ 26. ___ 27. ___ *Assertiveness* 15. ___ 34. ___	*Mood awareness* 1. ___ 6. ___ 13. ___ *Emotional creativity* 7. ___ 9. ___ 30. ___ *Optimism* 16. ___ *Passion/enthusiasm* 32. ___ 33. ___	*Empathy/respect* 17. ___ 19. ___ 21. ___ 25. ___ *Social responsibility* 20. ___ 24. ___ 29. ___ *Interpersonal relations* 10. ___ 11. ___ 12. ___ 14. ___ 22. ___ 23. ___ *Flexibility* 4. ___
Total: ___ 60	Total: ___ 45	Total: ___ 70

Plot your scores on the graph below. Connect the dots to familiarise yourself with your strengths and potential areas for growth in the three domains of emotionally intelligent behaviour.

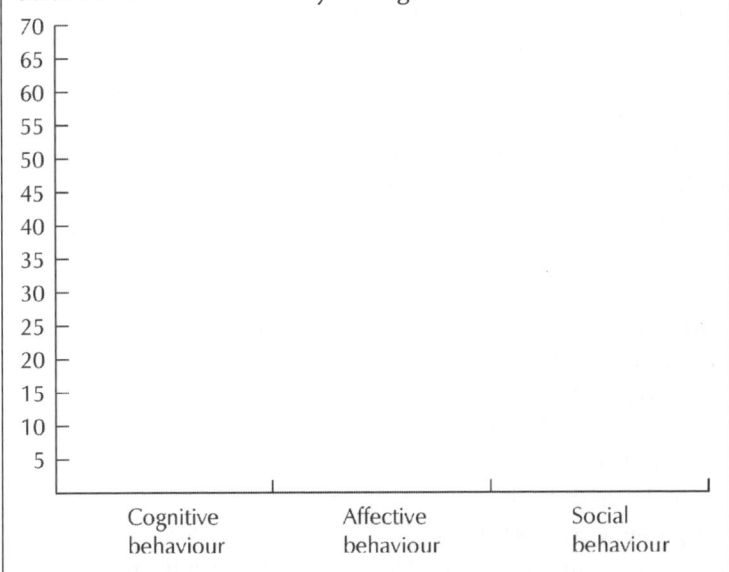

```
70
65
60
55
50
45
40
35
30
25
20
15
10
 5
      Cognitive      Affective      Social
      behaviour      behaviour      behaviour
```

Interpret your score

For the *cognitive* behavioural dimension you will score somewhere between 5 and 60, for the *affective* behavioural dimension between 5 and 45, and for the *social* behavioural dimension between 5 and 70 points. Circle any facet where your score was below 55 (on the *cognitive* dimension), below 40 (on the *affective* dimension) and below 65 (on the *social* dimension). This indicates a behavioural area that you can improve. Work through this book and resolve especially to practise the ideas and suggestions in each chapter. Your overall emotional intelligence will improve as you work on each area. Also take into consideration the role that your personality type plays in the strengths you have identified and the areas that you would like to improve.

Other opportunities for improvement can be found in any individual question from the checklist where you scored 4 or below. Circle those questions. A rating of 3 is average. So you need to target that area for improvement and turn it into a specific goal. If you have emotional intelligence, you are above average.

Effective teachers are generally high in all areas of emotionally intelligent behaviour. If you want your career and your relationship with your learners and others to soar, think of this as a workbook. Make a commitment to do something to improve your weaknesses (your undeveloped areas) each day. Use the ideas in each chapter and commit yourself to following the Ten Day Plan to Excellence in chapter 7.

Managing our emotions

Each situation ... presents us with choice. Which role will we play – teacher, student, rebel, counsellor, bully, introvert, rage-aholic, alcoholic, greedy, generous, peaceful, angry? Changing roles can be easier than changing our clothing, since all it takes is a change of perception, of attitude. It does, however, need a willingness to be aware of the roles we play as we go along.
(Marie T. Russell)

Understanding ourselves (our personality preferences and values system) is the first step in developing emotional intelligence. The next step is to learn how to recognise and manage our emotions, that is, to become more aware of how we feel. The secret of managing our emotions lies in recognising our feelings, particularly our negative or fear-based feelings. John Mulligan (1988) writes that knowing how to discriminate feelings is an acquired and learned skill. However, we need to have our feelings accepted and valued by ourselves and others before we can learn to distinguish them.

We are inundated with messages from others which tell us that our emotions are childish or shameful. The response to an expression of emotion is often one of alarm or embarrassment rather than respect and acceptance.

To avoid such censure we tend to hide our strong emotions under the veil of more acceptable ones, for example, boredom, embarrassment or tension. When we search a little deeper, we use techniques such as non-stop talking, laughter and physical stretching and yawning, the minute we encounter the stronger underlying emotions of anger, fear, grief, happiness and joy.

Emily Sterrett (2000) writes that if we do not pay attention to feelings and learn how to recognise and deal with them through better communication, they will reveal themselves in the body as fatigue, lack of concentration, pain or poor health. If we focus on emotions and allow ourselves to feel them, little by little, they will deepen in intensity and teach us to connect with others. Suppressing emotions, both the positive (love-based) and negative (fear-based) ones, denies our brains access to important natural chemicals. The alternative of prescription and illicit drugs is a poor substitute for the natural chemicals that are released through emotional experience and expression.

It's all a matter of choice

We can choose our behaviour when we wish to express emotions. Successful teachers employ seven strategies for an emotionally intelligent response to situations and events in the classroom. Let's take a closer look at these.

Strategy 1

They notice their *physiological response*, for example, a pounding heart, fast breathing, sweating palms or getting warm under the collar. They label the response. Sensitive teachers notice what emotion they are feeling from their non-verbal expression and they always remember that they do not have to verbalise or act on the emotion in any other way once they become aware of it.

Strategy 2

Teachers who manage their emotions well have learned to become aware of and to *differentiate* between the emotions they are experiencing. They realise the importance of *acknowledging* the emotions and do not try to ignore or deny them.

Strategy 3

Emotionally intelligent teachers apply *rational self-talk*, for example, "I know my idea has merit", "I am okay", "All is well".

Strategy 4

Emotionally intelligent teachers decide to *own their emotions*, that is, to accept full responsibility for feeling the way they do, by verbalising "I feel ..."

Strategy 5

They choose to allow themselves *time out* physically or mentally. For example, they engage in deep breathing or they take a walk. This gives them the opportunity to investigate their emotions and find out why they are responding in this way. Reflecting on their responses helps them to regain their inner calm and to respond in a socially responsible manner.

Strategy 6

When they feel calm enough, emotionally intelligent teachers *report* their emotions. They say what they are experiencing, for example, "I feel sad or angry about ..."

Strategy 7

Finally, emotionally intelligent teachers actively and assertively (firmly but gently) find ways to *resolve the issue* if possible. Happy teachers have learned how to manage their emotions well. They know the greatest secret of all: emotions should not be suppressed. Emotions should be observed, acknowledged, reported and dealt with in a socially responsible manner. They have learned how to take control of their emotional life and to harness their emotions wisely so as to improve their interactions with their learners and other people.

All emotion is reaction to opinion. In order to feel any emotion, positive or negative, you have to first have an opinion. Usually the way to go past it all is to change the opinion. In other words, life isn't necessarily going to go the way you want it. It's not necessarily going to be in this way, on that day, at this time, in that format, and so on ... The most important thing is to hang loose and go with the flow. (Stuart Wilde)

> **Try this now!**
>
> **Guidelines for developing your emotional intelligence**
>
> Start planning to improve your emotional intelligence skills by working through these guidelines.
>
> **Cognitive behaviour**
>
> - Accept that you are allowed to have emotions.
> - Notice the areas of tension in your body and notice how particular emotions affect your actions.
> - Verbalise the emotion by choosing the appropriate word to describe the intensity of the emotion you are experiencing.
> - Practise finding words to describe what and how you feel.
> - Lightly pepper your ordinary conversation with words which describe pleasant feelings and mildly difficult ones.
> - Share some of your warm emotions with others.
> - When you feel vulnerable, ask someone to listen and get the problem off your chest.
> - Recall the times when you felt really good about yourself. What specifically enabled you to achieve this state? Can you make use of these sources more effectively?
> - What blocks you from accepting yourself? Imagine this block: what does it look like? Draw it. Imagine you are the block. How do you feel? Imagine you have overcome the block. What does it feel like? Now converse with the block, playing both parts and negotiating until a workable compromise is agreed.
> - Learn to trust and accept your emotions. They provide valuable information about how you feel about yourself and what you need.
> - Listen to your body. Minor aches and pains, body temperature and illness can tell you what you are truly feeling.
> - Review your relationship with your body: How do you treat it? How do you feel about it? Do you get enough exercise? Do you have a healthy diet? The better you treat your body, the more you will respect yourself.
> - Try to be a friend to yourself and look after yourself. Give yourself love and appreciation when you feel yourself entering a negative cycle.
> - Start thinking differently about yourself and appreciate yourself on a daily basis. Take pride in your accomplishments and achievements, no matter how small.
> - Avoid people who put you down. Reinforce the positive messages you receive.
> - Tell yourself you are a caring, intelligent, attractive and worthy human being. Write these statements down and put them where you can see them every day.
>
> **Affective behaviour**
>
> - Learn breathing, relaxing and meditation techniques so that when you are under stress you can easily use them to control your emotions and responses.
> - Remove yourself from the stressful situation to recollect yourself.

- Change the subject to something you are more comfortable with to give you time to regain control of yourself.
- Focus on the positive aspects of what is going on, even if they are minor.
- Move around physically to unblock your energy, then proceed to do something constructive.
- Pour out your feelings into something creative.
- Gradually improve your physical fitness. You can then use vigorous exercise to do something useful when under stress.
- Learn deep meditation skills in which you can change the feelings into creative ideas.

Social behaviour
- Learn to focus on the impact of your ideas and actions on people.
- Learn to appreciate yourself and others unconditionally.
- Show appreciation for the input of others.
- Make an effort to take an interest in the well-being of those who work closely with you or those who are important to you in your life.
- Learn to open up and share your concerns with others.
- Solicit feedback and suggestions from others to attain team goals.
- Give your undivided attention and listen actively when communicating with others.
- Encourage, praise, appreciate and affirm the ideas and efforts of others.
- Celebrate the ideas, appearance, values and behaviour that contribute towards team goals.
- Be genuine and honest in expressing care and concern.
- Touch supportively and in a nurturing way.
- Share your own strengths and weaknesses.
- Offer help and assistance when needed.
- Identify with others through emotional empathy.

Balance your thinking and feeling mind
- State the exact meaning of the words you use. Do not assume you have the same experience in mind as someone else when you use a word.
- Learn to ask the right questions or formulate a problem in a way that makes it easier to solve.
- Brainstorm what you already know of the problem/challenge.
- Prioritise alternatives or solutions.
- Analyse: Discriminate between facts and fiction. Examine pros and cons.
- Be non-judgmental. Accept yourself and other people as they are, rather than push them to what they should be.
- Have a support group with whom you can share your intuitive/visionary explorations.
- Keep a journal of intuitive/creative ideas.

- Take time to reflect and identify your feelings and values when making decisions.
- Look beyond quick fixes, plan ahead and consider the wider ramifications.
- Consider all sides before deciding, including the human factor.
- Develop a future-oriented perspective when generating solutions.
- Pay attention to the people aspects of a situation or decision.
- Bring joy and passion into your daily activities, no matter how important they seem. Be enthusiastic about being alive.

Managing difficult behaviour creatively

Teachers often have to deal with problematic learner behaviour. Dealing with difficult behaviour in the classroom should not be confused with discipline. Discipline is a process by which teachers help learners learn from mistakes and improve their behaviour and academic performance. Conflicts, disagreements or non-compliant behaviour are generally sparked off or triggered by some idiosyncratic behaviour on the part of the difficult or non-compliant learner.

Difficult learner behaviour is usually the result of communication or co-operation that went wrong between teacher and learners. It may also be the result of punitive methods used to discipline learners. Although difficult behaviour is often interpreted as sheer stubbornness, in reality it may be an expression of fear or anxiety on the part of the learner. The difficulty may also be caused by a conflict over values or a difference in personality type. Conflicts and disagreements are dysfunctional when they result in aggression or establish negative patterns of behaviour in learners.

Emotionally intelligent teachers use eight strategies to deal with difficult learner behaviour:

Strategy 1

They recognise and acknowledge how they are feeling. They know they do not have to express this or act on it.

Strategy 2

They stop what they are doing and play for time to calm their thoughts and emotions. For example, they breathe deeply and count to ten. They know that they do not have to respond immediately. They avoid being forced into a destructive response by their own compulsion to act or from outside pressure.

Strategy 3

They recognise that it is ignorance and inability or a message of some deeper emotional need causing the conflict rather than intention on the part of the difficult learner.

Strategy 4

They control their response by managing their emotions. They do not get taken in by learners' behaviour and overreact. They avoid accusing, belittling or threatening learners. They are aware of the body language they project, for example, aggression or openness.

Strategy 5

They determine their values and goals. They work out what they need to get from the situation and how important it is to them.

Strategy 6

They level with learners by engaging in a dialogue, for example, in one-to-one situations or in a group. Dialogue means learners are allowed to state their point of view. Emotionally intelligent teachers also show respect for learners' views, desires and feelings. They hear them out and listen with their hearts to determine the emotional needs that are behind the viewpoints and behaviour.

Strategy 7

They make learners aware of the impact of their behaviour and negotiate a compromise or a solution to the issue at hand.

Strategy 8

They stand firm and declare the boundaries and limits. However, they remain flexible and are willing to compromise when needs and values clash.

Emotionally intelligent teachers do not view misconduct and confrontational behaviour of learners as a personal affront. They avoid engaging in power struggles with learners. Instead, they wait until a time when the interaction will be calmer and more constructive.

In this chapter we explored how a teacher's emotional intelligence (as expressed in his or her behavioural style) should assert itself interactively in the classroom to promote a classroom climate that facilitates optimal teaching and learning. Our emotions are the foundation for creativity, passion, optimism, drive and transformation. A thought without emotion falls flat; it is the emotion attached to the thought that produces the energy for action.

Emotionally intelligent teachers do not let the presence of emotions in the classroom scare them. Instead, they have learned to harness their energy for improving their teaching and the performance of learners. Furthermore, they are motivated:

they radiate enthusiasm, initiative and persistence in finding ways to improve their interaction with their learners and other people. Simply put, they have mastered the art of being emotionally intelligent. You can too, if you want to improve. When you have learned how to use your rational brain to balance your emotional brain, nothing can stop you.

> **! Try this now!**
>
> 1. Reflect on the learners in your classroom whom you find difficult. Write down their names. Visualise each learner, including their behaviour, the setting in which the behaviour occurs, their attitude and their speech.
> 2. Note how the behaviour affects you. What are your thoughts, your feelings and your own behaviour with regard to the learner?
> 3. How do you respond to each learner and each behaviour? Is your response avoidance, attack, sarcasm, anxiety or punitive?
> 4. Do you notice any patterns emerging regarding the kind of learner you find difficult, the specific behaviour or the setting? Does your response vary? What do you find useful about this information?
> 5. Repeat the exercise from the learners' perspective. Which learners find you difficult? What do they find difficult about you? How does it affect them? How do they respond?
> 6. Was it easier to define your difficult learners or to define what learners find difficult about you? Was there similarity or overlap in the answers to both?
>
> Check your answers with the learners involved to gain more reliable information.

> **▶ Taking action!**
>
> *Three suggestions to put the ideas in this chapter into practice:*
>
> 1. Reflect on your emotional intelligence profile. Look at your strengths and note how these behaviours influence the classroom climate. Look at your weaker areas. Try to determine how these areas impact on the behaviour of learners and the general classroom atmosphere. List ideas for improving your responses to particularly difficult learner behaviour.
> 2. Study the characteristics of your personality preference (thinking or feeling). How do these characteristics relate to your emotional intelligence strengths and weaknesses? List ideas for developing your least preferred function. Use the guidelines on balancing your thinking and feeling minds.
> 3. Review your values profile and personal values statement in chapter 3. See if you can find a link between your personality preference (thinking or feeling), your emotional intelligence profile and your values. Identify the areas that need to be developed. What new behaviours or attitude will you need to improve your overall emotional intelligence?

Review questions

1. Explain the term emotional intelligence. How would you describe the emotionally intelligent teacher? Give an outline of the emotional intelligence profile of such a teacher.
2. Describe the basic emotional intelligence competencies that teachers need to develop.
3. Is it important for teachers to display emotionally intelligent behaviour in the classroom? Give reasons for your answer.
4. How does self-esteem influence our ability to display emotionally intelligent behaviour? (Review chapter 1.)
5. Does personality type influence our ability to display emotionally intelligent behaviour? Give reasons for your answer.
6. What guidelines would you give to a teacher who struggles to manage emotions?
7. How would you manage a disruptive learner in the classroom? Give reasons for your answer.

✓ In a snapshot

1. Emotional intelligence describes the ability to perceive, to integrate, to understand and reflectively manage our own and other people's emotions. It includes the extent to which we are able to tap into our feelings and emotions as a source of energy to guide our thinking and actions, as well as our cognitive ability to manage our emotional life with greater or lesser skill.
2. Emotionally intelligent teachers display a unique set of competencies (knowledge, skills and attitudes) which enable them to manage their emotional life more effectively and to achieve their life goals.
3. We are emotionally creative when we are able to use our emotional state to create harmonious conditions and achieve an inner sense of well-being and happiness – the secret of happy teachers.
4. Our personality preferences influence our ability to demonstrate emotionally intelligent behaviour.
5. Emotionally intelligent teachers apply their emotional skills and creativity in the way they manage difficult classroom behaviour.

Suggested reading

Bar-On, R. (1997) *BarOn Emotional Quotient Inventory: A Measure of Emotional Intelligence – User's Manual.* Toronto, ON: Multi-Health Systems

Cobb, CD. & Mayer, JD. (2000) 'Emotional intelligence: What the research says' *Educational Leadership*, 58 (3): 14–18

Gerson, RF. (2000) 'The emotional side of performance improvement' *Performance Improvement*, 39 (8): 18–23

Goldsworthy, R. (2000) 'Designing instruction for emotional intelligence' *Educational Technology*, 40 (5): 43–48

Hirsh, S. & Kummerow, J. (1989) *Life Types.* New York: Warner Books

Mather, N. & Goldstein, S. (2001) *Learning Disabilities and Challenging Behaviours.* Illinois: Paul H. Brookes Publishing Co

Mayer, JD. & Salovey, P. (1997) 'What is emotional intelligence: Implications for educators' in P. Salovey & D. Sluyter (editors) *Emotional Development, Emotional Literacy, and Emotional Intelligence: Educational Implications.* New York: Basic Books

Sterret, EA. (2000) *The Manager's Pocket Guide to Emotional Intelligence.* Amherst, MA: HRD Press

Chapter 5: Nurturing the child that hurts

In chapter 4, we discussed the emotional intelligence profile of successful teachers. This chapter takes a closer look at why adults find emotional intelligence hard.

When we grow up we receive messages from parents, teachers, caregivers and peers that affect our self-esteem. These messages are both positive and negative. They shape our self-image.

A child is innocent and like an empty vessel waiting to be filled with knowledge, skills and awareness of the laws and workings of the world. A child is also vulnerable and in need of guidance and safe boundaries from adults who seem to be wiser and stronger. Children depend on their parents, teachers and caregivers to set a good example and to firmly but lovingly guide them on the path towards self-sufficiency. Children are haunted throughout their lives by the beliefs, values and messages imposed upon them, if they cannot consciously release or transform them into empowering beliefs, values and thoughts.

Children absorb and internalise the positive and negative messages they receive. These messages become a lasting part of their lives. Unfortunately, many messages focus on what is not good about us and lower our self-esteem.

Sometimes early nurturance needs are not sufficiently met by early childhood caregivers, parents and teachers. Research suggests that when our emotional and spiritual needs are not adequately met in the first four to six years, we lose the connection to our talented true Self (also called the Spirit within us). The true Self contains the seed of potential for what we can be and achieve in life. On the other hand, we construct a false self to protect ourselves.

The true Self is that aspect of ourselves that is not anxious or wounded. It is the Self with open heart and mind. The false self is that aspect of us that cannot trust, our fear-based feelings and unfulfilled emotional needs.

*I do not ask for any crown
But that which all may win;
Nor try to conquer any world
Except the one within.
(Louisa May Alcott)*

Figure 5.1 The true Self and the false self

The wounded false self

Children are particularly susceptible to receiving and believing negative messages. These messages devalue us and lead us to believe that we are not worthwhile. If we are not given considerable acceptance and understanding by those we look up to, we assume that there is something wrong with us. Because we are open and vulnerable as children, we develop ways of defending ourselves by constructing a false self. This happens when we do not receive the emotional support and attention necessary to develop our true Self.

John Mulligan (1988) wrote that the false self is a mask or a front that we present to the world to protect our true Self. The false self is also called the adapted self, since the true Self is adapted to conform to the expectations and desires of others. This is done to gain love from those who are important for our survival: parents, teachers and caregivers. The adapted self masks our feelings of guilt, shame, hurt, anger and fear.

As children we believe that we are to blame for the behaviour of our parents, teachers and caregivers. Hence, we develop the emotional wounds of guilt, shame, hurt, anger and fear. Childhood wounds remain unconsciously buried deep within the psyche. Later in life, we re-enact through our false self the dramas of our childhood in our relationships with other adults and children. Unless we consciously heal the unintended psychological damage we suffered as children, we are bound to set ourselves up for more of the same.

The true Self cannot ever be totally buried. We are often aware that it is inside us somewhere. However, because our self-image is bound up with the adaptive self, we are not fully in touch with our true talented Self. As long as we try to live up to and by the standards and expectations of others, we will feel that we are not what we should be. This pretence results in feelings of anxiety, shame, anger, hate and sadness. We have learned to suppress these feelings deep within ourselves.

Consequently, the false self is also called the wounded inner child. This is primarily because of the deep emotional wounds (suppressed guilt, shame, hurt, anger and fear) that are buried deep down. As children we could not or were too scared to speak out our confusion, anger or hurt. Adults who have not released and healed these emotional wounds, become what we call Grown Wounded Children.

What wound have you left unhealed? Are you willing to begin healing today? An unhealed wound drains you of the very energy needed to live beyond the wound. (Iyanla Vanzant)

Table 5.1 Attributes of wounded inner children

scared child	lonely child
humble child	selfish child
contented child	loving child
orphan child	jealous child
judgemental child	sad child
shamed child	playful child
guilty child	aggressive child
good child	defiant child

> ! **Try this now!**
>
> Do you present a false self (the wounded inner child) to others? Answer the questions in the self-assessment honestly.
>
> If you have answered mostly 'Yes', then you definitely have a wounded inner child that you need to nurture and heal.

Checklist	Yes/No
1. Do you blame others and become angry, make excuses or deny your behaviour instead of taking responsibility for your actions?	
2. Do you endeavour to fulfill your duties and obligations in a timely and appropriate manner with a joyful attitude?	
3. Do you resent your responsibilities and see them as a burden instead of an opportunity to support and serve those around you?	
4. Do you express your appreciation to those who serve you in return?	
5. Do you still believe that for you to be right, someone else must be wrong?	
6. How often do you fall into the role of childish, irresponsible behaviour?	

7. Are you still acting or interacting in some old conditioned childish ways?
8. Are you willing to let go of the painful experiences of the past and assume the strengths and wisdom your parents have portrayed to you?
9. Are you still looking for love and approval outside of you, that is, seeking it from others, and thus struggling to find it within yourself, that is, loving yourself unconditionally?
10. Do you always go to extremes to please others, hoping they will approve of you and love you?
11. Are you scared to speak out your point of view because you fear rejection or abandonment by others?
12. Are you sensitive to whether you receive recognition from others for your work and actions?
13. Do you often feel lonely and that you do not belong or fit in?
14. Are you scared to set clear boundaries because you fear others will reject you?
15. Do you tend to judge and criticise others for their flaws to show they are not good enough?
16. Do you find it difficult to trust other people?
17. Do you find it difficult to be emotionally close with others?
18. Do you tend to feel guilty when someone criticises your behaviour or when you have to reprimand them about the appropriateness of their behaviour?
19. Do feel deeply ashamed of yourself when you have made a mistake?
20. Are you always satisfied to be the one who is overlooked/receive less or do you constantly demand other people's attention?

The Grown Wounded Child

Grown Wounded Children are adults who survive *unintended* emotional and spiritual deprivation by their early childhood caregivers, parent and teachers. The developmental impact of a low nurturance environment steadily accumulates and self-amplifies. Nurturance deprivations range from minor everyday neglect, for example, lack of loving facial expressions, eye-contact, touching, soothing, calming sounds; to nutritional, stimulation and knowledge deficiencies; to major trauma like abuse and psychological or physical abandonment.

Grown Wounded Children bear emotional wounds like excessive shame, guilt, fears and major reality distortions. They distrust problems. They could have difficulty bonding with some or all people. This is disguised as moderate or great social and professional success, and/or punctuated by a series of hidden or obvious, financial, scholastic and/or occupational failure.

Since they are unseen, these childhood wounds seem normal but cause stress and strain in our adult lives. They affect our relationships, careers, parenting, teaching, physical and mental health.

Unresolved and unhealed childhood wounds affect our ability as adults to have emotionally intelligent interactions with other people and our learners. The emotional wounds form blockages to being in touch with our true ability to express ourselves in appropriate and healthy ways.

Children who grow up in high nurturance environments where they receive unconditional acceptance, respect, genuineness, empathy, guidance and safe boundaries are more apt to develop their true Self. They are able to make effective, heart-head balanced (or emotionally intelligent) decisions. They grow up to be adults with a healthy self-esteem and the confidence to be successful in their relationships and careers.

The effects of false self dominance

Research by Peter Gerlach (2006) indicates that many adults unconsciously suffer from false self wounds. However, they are unaware of how much their well-meaning false self is controlling them and how this is affecting their own and their children's lives.

When we allow ourselves to be dominated by the false self, we unconsciously attract significantly wounded partners, with painful results. The interaction of wounds in two people ruled by their false self causes mounting relationship conflict and stress and promotes eventual psychological or legal break-up. This is likely to happen if both people lack basic information on effective relationships and emotionally intelligent communication. Often divorced Grown Wounded Children have to deal with a web of unfinished issues with ex-partners and even parents or family. This complicates their potential for new primary relationships.

Wounded people in effective personal recovery (often in midlife) begin to choose wholistically healthier, high nurturance settings and relationships. Over time, the quality of their own and their children's lives and interactions improves notably.

Grown Wounded Children who have not tried to develop emotional intelligence and progress from their childhood wounds towards personal recovery, unintentionally choose and promote low nurturance family environments. Consequently, the result is that they pass on false self wounds to their children, in spite of their fervent vows not to be like their own (neglectful or abusive) mom or dad.

The same is seen in wounded childhood caregivers. As children they could show negative symptoms of false self dominance and act out, get sick, very angry, withdrawn, over anxious, hyper or depressed before puberty. On the other hand, they could try to adapt to their nurturance deprivations and false self injuries by becoming *super* responsible and obedient or being relentlessly helpful and cheerful. This is usually an unconscious survival tactic and not necessarily wholistic health or happiness.

Recovering from our childhood wounds

Recovery is a long-term process because wounding spans decades (30 to 45 years) during which we accumulate intolerable pain and weariness. This is accompanied by ineffective attempts to deny, ignore and relieve the wounding. People generally need to hit rock bottom before they break their lifelong denials. This tends to happen at midlife. However, there is no need to wait that long. With emotional intelligence and a conscious decision to manage our feelings every day, we can recover from childhood wounding at a much younger age.

True wound recovery means realising, grieving over and accepting that our childhood lacked major emotional and spiritual nurturance. As old denials dissolve, we learn to process suppressed feelings of hurt, rage, and ultimately, deep sadness because the caregivers we depended on could not or did not know how to meet our development needs adequately.

Recovery could awaken the need to confront older family members so as to release long-suppressed feelings. The reaction of parents or relatives could range from family-wide recovery (in the best case); to major guilt, sadness and depression; to rigid, angry rejection, criticism and hostility as expressed in words like, "How dare you accuse Mom and me of being inadequate or wounded parents after all that we did for you!" Adults who successfully recover from childhood wounds enjoy the following ten characteristics:

1. They have forgiven their parents and caregivers.
2. They have taken down the mask of moral superiority.
3. They have taken full responsibility for their feelings, thoughts and actions.
4. They have learned to embrace the wounded inner child in themselves and others.
5. They look at the strengths and weaknesses they have developed.
6. They have brought love to the wounded parts of their hearts and mind.
7. They have surrended their victimhood as a grown wounded child.
8. They have accepted the truth of their being, their true, talented self and the spirit within.
9. They have learned to walk through their own darkness and, therefore, they are able to live from their true self.
10. They have learned to trust their heart and mind.

Forgiving parents or caregivers

They have searched deep within themselves for the lessons and wisdom learned from parents or other caregivers. They have come to realise that we are all (including parents, caregivers, children) filled with unspeakable wounds. They know that behaviour is driven by unacknowledged pain, guilt, shame and fear embedded in our wounds. They believe that their parents and caregivers did the best they knew, just as we all try to do.

Removing the mask of moral superiority

They have allowed the boy or girl within them to look out at the boy or girl in others. They understand that love and acceptance starts within their own heart, that forgiveness has its roots in an open and willing heart.

Being fully responsible for feelings, thoughts and actions

They understand that it is futile to blame others and become angry, make excuses for or deny their own behaviour. They no longer mask the wounds within.

Embracing the wounded inner children within themselves and others

Beneath the mask of vicious anger, depression, unkind words and actions they see the boy or girl who does not believe they are lovable. They are conscious and aware of their behaviour and feelings. They make every effort to give others the loving support, guidance and acceptance they were not given.

Developing strengths and awareness

They consciously examine their relationships and evaluate whether they are growing or stagnating and caught up in inertia as they replay the same old scenes of their life over and over again. They set boundaries and clearly state the framework in which they intend to operate and what they expect from those around them.

Loving the wounded parts of mind and heart

They have allowed themselves to be loved and nurtured and brought healing to their deepest feeling of hurt and betrayal. They have reclaimed their power for themselves and have reconnected with their true innocent Self.

Surrendering victimhood as a Grown Wounded Child

Therefore, they can no longer be treated unfairly. They understand that they are the very source of love, kindness, empathy, respect, acceptance and forgiveness. They know that it all begins with and ends with them.

Accepting the true talented Self and the Spirit within

The darkness of their childhood wounds have disappeared.

Living from their true Self

They do not deny the darkness of their emotional wounds, they walk through it. There is nothing about themselves or anyone else that they are afraid to look at and the darkness of their past trauma has no more hold over them. They are able to release the false self and present the true Self to the world.

Trusting mind and heart

By embracing their feelings they have given wings to all that is real and true within themselves, the true source of happiness.

When we follow the journey to recovery, there is no more resentment or grievances. There is no anticipation of attack. There is no guilt or perception of punishment. There is just the innocence of our true Self and the promise of a life lived in joy.

Our emotions are the key. They send us messages through our bodies to tell us when we are out of balance or repressing past wounds. The emotions of our childhood wounds remind us that the wounds are locked up within us. They keep on prompting us to be released. Until we awake from our slumber and consciously put a stop to the old scenes of our lives, we will keep re-enacting the wounded dramas of our childhood. Emotional intelligence recognises the gift of our emotions in helping us to return to wholeness and health.

Emotional intelligence means we live from the inside out and risk being our true Selves. It allows us to move towards our greatest joy. The spirit of others (including our learners) cannot be uplifted unless we learn to trust our emotional intelligence and share it unconditionally with the world. Emotional intelligence helps us to move towards joy and that is the greatest secret of truly happy teachers.

Take the word victim off from your person – out of your vocabulary. It reeks with the old energy and does not suit your magnificence.
(Kryon)

> **! Try this now!**
>
> **Assess your development needs**
>
> Which developmental needs did you have to fill to live as an independent adult? Did you receive competent help with them? What about the children and learners whom you care for? How are they doing with each of these vital needs?
>
> 1. Think critically, objectively, clearly and independently to make effective everyday decisions.
> 2. Be clearly aware of and balance dynamic emotions, thoughts, intuitions and current needs to react to life's challenges in healthy, safe and satisfying ways.
> 3. Monitor and control your bubble of empathetic awareness away from focusing on your own current needs and thoughts, towards including others at times.
> 4. Forge a realistic identity to satisfy the primal questions of:
>   - Who am I?
>   - How am I like or different from my parents, other people or others of my gender?
> 5. Forge genuine self-respect, self-trust and self-awareness, as the foundation for meeting your short and long-term needs effectively.
> 6. Communicate effectively (in an emotionally intelligent way) with other people in both calm and conflictual settings.
> 7. Learn to understand, appreciate and effectively care for your changing body, to promote ongoing health and healing.
> 8. Form safe emotional attachments to bond with selected people, ideas and principles; know how to grieve well when such bonds break up.
> 9. Practise effective social and relationship skills like tact, empathy, intimacy, trust, assertion, co-operation, obedience and respectful confrontation, to get along well with other people.
> 10. Take authentic responsibility for the outcomes of your decisions and behaviour.
> 11. Evolve meaningful answers to the core life questions about spirituality and religion, life and our origins, destiny and fate, good and evil, death.
> 12. Learn from and adjust to personal mistakes or failures and be emotionally resilient.
> 13. Evolve an authentic framework of ethics and morals to discern right from wrong and good from bad.
> 14. Successfully earn, save, spend and responsibly manage money.
> 15. Make responsible, healthy young adult decisions about sex and childhood conception; acquire fundamental ideas about childhood development and effective parenting.
> 16. Acknowledge that you have a unique, worthy life mission and purpose.
> 17. Evolve a meaningful plan about where your life is going in the next few years.
> 18. Promptly ask for and accept human and spiritual help, without guilt, shame and anxiety when life becomes chaotic and overwhelming.
> 19. Accurately discern who and what to trust; how to adapt to people, ideas and circumstances you do no trust enough.
> 20. Live comfortably with ambiguity and uncertainty.

Table 5.2 The journey to recovery

To truly heal the wounded child within, allow the pain to come up
■ Feel the pain. Remember the violation. ■ Forgive yourself. ■ Be kind to yourself. ■ See the perpetrator's pain. ■ See the attack as a call for love. ■ Stand up for yourself now. ■ Vow never to be a victim again. ■ Vow never to betray yourself again. ■ Understand you accepted the pain because you wanted love and did not know how to get it. ■ Say what you want now. ■ Say no to violation. ■ Learn to say no to what you do not want. ■ Learn to say yes to what you do want. ■ Do not confuse the two. ■ Do not accept what does not feel good. ■ Tell the truth, even if it means that others leave. ■ Be firm. Be clear. Get on with your life. ■ Be willing to feel your emotions and to let others know how you feel. Own what you feel and do not make others responsible for it. Blame is not appropriate here, neither for you nor anyone else. ■ Know that healing is a lifelong process. More and more layers of abandonment, rejection and shame will come up. It is okay. You know you may feel the pain and move through it. Have confidence in your healing journey. ■ You need not go looking for the darkness. It will come to you all by itself. Once you are willing to heal, the pain of the broken self automatically comes up. ■ Be patient. You cannot rush the process. Your healing has its own gentle pace. Stay with it. Do not push too hard or you will revert to fear and freeze up. Just be willing to deal with each issue in the present moment. *(Based on Ferrini, 1996)*

Hear the voice of the inner critic

Just as fears and anxieties can get in the way of success, so can the bad feelings of self-judgement and criticism (the voice of our inner critic) also hold us back. Nothing weakens or derails us as effectively as the sting of negative self-evaluation. There are two main mental processes to put ourselves down:
1. Making internal pictures of failing or messing up; and
2. Hearing an internal voice (our inner critic) saying what we are doing wrong.

The inner critic acts as a guardian for the false self. It fills our conscious mind with detailed descriptions of our flaws, failings, mistakes and stupidity. If the inner critic is not moderated by our true Self, our resident shamed, guilty and/or scared inner child activates and floods us with intense feelings and thoughts.

The inner critic distrusts and takes over the true Self. It lives in a traumatic, unsafe past. It wants to protect us from being harmed like we were in childhood.

The negative internal messages we receive from our inner critic do not come in isolation. They are part of a pattern and invariably linked with the past. A pattern arises when one incident triggers off a whole range of emotions, behaviours and actions which cause us to feel out of control. This happens automatically and we may be aware of thinking, "There, I've done it again. Why am I doing this?"

If, for example, we were told as a child, either explicitly or tacitly, that we are not creative, this could have been painful. Now, if people ask us to do something creative or criticise us when we try to be creative, that pain will resurface and trigger off a pattern of feelings.

When we fall into the pattern, we could have a range of responses. We may become defensive, aggressive, depressed or low in energy. We may feel worthless or inferior and overcompensate by being boastful.

If we accept negative messages from the inner critic and denigrate ourselves, we are less likely to tolerate the success and good news of other people, even our learners.

Part of the journey to recovery is to gradually convince the well-meaning inner critic and guardian that it is safe to moderate its criticism and protect the inner child from stress. However, you want to live in the present time and rely on the true Self to keep you safe each day. This will reduce the crippling wounds of excessive shame and guilt.

Emotional intelligence offers five vital strategies to break the destructive internal messages from the well-meaning inner critic:

Strategy 1 Be aware of the internal voice of your critical self

Know that past messages about yourself have caused you distress. Stop for a minute and think about what the inner critic is saying. Notice any communication concerning your emotions, your body or your abilities.

Strategy 2 Discover the intention of this critical voice

Ask what it is trying to do for you that is positive. The inner critic acts as a guardian, a protector for the wounded inner child. It wants to accomplish something positive for the inner child. Therefore, find out what that positive intention is. Ask the voice:

"What's your intention for me?"

"What are you trying to accomplish for me?"

Common answers to these questions are, for example:

"I'm trying to keep you from making a fool of yourself."

"I want to protect you."

"I'm making sure you do what is right."

After you hear an answer from this voice, notice your response to the intention. If you have difficulty accepting that what you hear is positive, keep asking the voice until you do find an intention you can agree with. For instance, if the voice says:

"I'm trying to get you motivated."

You can then ask:

"And when you are trying to get me motivated, what does that do for me?"

The voice might say:

"Well, when you are motivated, you get things done and make more money."

To this you might respond:

"And when I'm getting things done and making more money, what does that do for me?"

Then the voice might answer:

"You'll be a success and feel good about yourself."

That is an intention most of us certainly appreciate.

Strategy 3 Acknowledge and thank the inner critic

Once you have determined the positive intention of the inner critic, you need to affirm that you value its intention. Say:

"I'm glad you have this positive intention for me. Thank you, for wanting this for me."

When you do this, you have achieved a crucially important step, because both you and the voice agree on the positive intention. You are no longer adversaries. Now you are allies who can work together to resolve the initial problem. A nagging and criticising voice can cause you to fail. This is the reverse of its positive intention, which is to help you succeed.

Strategy 4 Negotiate with your inner critic

Now that you and the inner critic both agree on the positive intention, you can now explore more comfortable and efficient ways to get the results you both want. Here is an example of how this process works:

> One night Gugu complained that lately she was a bit blue and depressed. As she explored the issue, she discovered an internal voice saying, "You are a bad person." When she asked the voice, "What is your intention in saying that?" the response was, "I want to get you to pay attention to how you come across to others. You've been really negative towards others lately, and you should stop doing that."
>
> Gugu was surprised at the answer. Yet, when she thought about it, she could verify that the voice was right. She had been negative towards others recently. She responded, "And when I stop being negative towards others, what will that do for me?" The answer was, "You'll have more self-respect and feel better about yourself. You will be positive towards others and the result of that is more friends and better relationships."
>
> Gugu considered this all to be valuable information. She realised that she had gravitated towards habitually noticing what was wrong in her life and the lives of others. She realised how much value there was in having a voice that wanted her to feel self-respect so that she could improve her relationships with others.

Strategy 5 Generate new behaviours

Take the example of Gugu: she moved on to asking the voice if it would be interested in additional behavioural choices to get the positive intention met besides telling her, "You're a bad person" which actually made the problem worse. After getting agreement to that, she had the critic's creative part generate ideas of new behaviours for her to do.

The three choices that the voice liked and agreed to were to breathe deeply and smile before responding to others; to notice and comment on the positive that the other person is doing; and to offer encouragement to Gugu about what she herself was doing well, noticing the positive aspects of her own behaviour. At the conscious level, Gugu realised that these choices would certainly work much better for her than an internal voice that was critical or judgemental.

Emotional intelligence needs constant practice. As with all the exercises in this book, the more often we practise them, the more they will become an automatic part of our thinking and responding.

Implications for teachers

Mr Webster asks his Grade 12 learners to open their exercise books to discuss the homework. He cannot believe his ears when the learners tell him that he never gave them any homework. This is so unusual that the learners think it is a bit of a joke and chuckle at the idea. But not so Mr Webster, who feels he has lost face irretrievably as a result of his slip-up and that the learners are taking unfair advantage by laughing at him. Being thus caught off-guard he momentarily loses his cool because he is burdened by responsibility and his hidden fear of not being able to measure up.

His habitually calm and professionally correct demeanour suddenly gives way to an apparently inexplicable and irrational outburst of epic dimensions to everybody's, not least his own, amazement and dismay. He says, "I hate being humiliated like this! Yes, laugh, you fools! What do you know about the hardships of being a teacher. Nothing! Nothing! I'm sick and tired of you! So, from now on you don't have to do homework and I hope you fail at the end of the year! So there, why should I worry about your lives!"

Mr Webster starts swearing, he throws his books on the desk and informs the learners that he is finished with his profession. After slamming the door, the learners realise that their highly respected teacher has lost it. They stare at the door, confused and startled.

The following day, to their surprise, Mr Webster apologised for his behaviour by saying that there is no excuse for bad behaviour. "Sorry class, I am going through a very difficult period in my life. Will you forgive me for overreacting? One thing I can say today, though, is that I need you. I love being a teacher and I do want you to succeed. You know that I feel for you." To Mr Webster's amazement, this act of contrition elicits a spontaneous standing ovation from the learners and leaves him completely vindicated. On behalf of the class, one of the learners declares, "Don't worry, Sir! We'll all work together and pull our weight – really! And you'll see, we will make it."

Mr Webster's expression of real feeling and passion for his profession, as well as his interest in his learners won them over as no amount of carping or begging could ever have done.

Teachers who are unconsciously dominated by their false selves, find it difficult to create a high nurturance, emotionally warm classroom environment. Unintentionally, they create the low nurturance environment that they themselves were exposed to as children. At a subconscious level act out or model the behaviour of their own early childhood caregivers.

Unless they consciously become aware of the cause and effect of their false self behaviour, they will unfortunately and unintentionally re-enact their childhood dramas in the classroom. Worse still, they will transfer their unhealed wounds onto the learners who look up to them as role models and figures of authority.

Teachers who make a conscious effort to develop their emotional intelligence are aware of how their suppressed emotions affect their behaviour and stress levels. They are aware of how they react towards their learners. They take greater responsibility for their emotions and, in time, learn greater emotional self-control.

A high nurturance classroom environment fosters an open mind and heart (see chapter 3). It empowers learners on their journey of self-understanding and self-appreciation. It is an environment where they can share ideas without being judged or preached at.

Teachers cannot foster open-heartedness if they exclude anyone from the group or give preferential treatment to certain children. Learners open their hearts and minds when they feel welcome or treated as equals. Nothing shuts down the heart and mind quicker than competition for love and attention. Many people, including teachers and learners, have deep emotional wounds. They react quickly and defensively to the slightest hint of unfairness, even if unintentional.

Therefore, the primary focus of the classroom environment must be to establish the high nurturance conditions described in chapter 3, namely, the general teacher demeanour of genuineness, respect, empathy, passion, enthusiasm, unconditional acceptance of and interest in the learners; setting clear boundaries that create psychological safety; having a positive self-image, nurturing feelings of belonging; promoting purposeful behaviour; and developing a sense of personal competence.

Learners must each be given the chance to be heard. They should be encouraged not to suppress feelings or hide them from others. When a safe, loving, non-judgemental space is created in which feelings can be expressed without attack or blame, misunderstandings, judgements and the projection of individual emotional wounds can be dissolved. Teachers and learners return to their hearts and bodies. Calmness and harmony

---

Pull divine love out of the bag of your own personal energy and face yourself in a forgiving way. Forgive the child inside.
(Kryon)

Offer your learners experiences of safe emotional bonding. Give them hope. Give them love and acceptance. Nobody gives love without receiving it. Nobody gives a gift he/she does not simultaneously receive.

are restored. Trust is re-established. Emotionally intelligent teachers understand that we want to find love and acceptance, so they do not hesitate to offer this to their learners.

What to do when the buttons are pushed

Because we need love and acceptance, we tend to explode in rage, attacking or humiliating others when their behaviour or words trigger our childhood wounds. When this happens, successful teachers use their emotional intelligence and apply the six effective strategies:

1. Take responsibility for your thoughts and feelings.
2. Do not project.
3. Listen without interrupting.
4. Do not allow yourself to be cut off or steamrollered. Ask that you be heard in the same way as you listened.
5. Do not attack.
6. Do not defend. Just ask for equal time. By not making the other person wrong, but insisting on equality, anger is diffused. Thus, learners receive a living demonstration of emotional intelligence at work.

Feel the pain of others. Understand their struggles and disappointments, their hardships and inadequacies and open your heart to them. Realise that everyone is doing the best they possibly can. Judge no one. But rather, cradle all of humanity in your heart. (Daniel Levin)

To apply these strategies, teachers must be skillful and practised in emotional intelligence. Through their ability to model emotionally intelligent behaviour, the entire class learns how to behave in a socially responsible way. They see that even the most difficult situation can be resolved so that everyone is honoured.

Emotional intelligence shows us how to live with the false self, the wounded inner child when it starts talking. We learn how to be with our inner child, to acknowledge it within ourselves and our learners, and to let it go. The key is to keep on practising the skills of emotional intelligence.

The secret to emotional intelligence is not to stop ourselves from having judgements or feelings, such as anger, sadness, hurt and shame. Rather, we need to be aware of our judgements (the voice of the inner critic) and feelings. We should look at them, listen to their messages, and then let go of them. If we practise this, we become more relaxed and open.

The false self will always try to protect us from the hurt, anger, fear, rage, shame and sadness that we keep buried within. By confessing these feelings to ourselves and others, we release them even more powerfully than we can by ourselves. We establish a climate in which the false self (the wounded child) is acknowledged as a natural phenomenon for all people. The wounded child comes and goes, sometimes with anger, sometimes with sadness.

Emotional intelligence skills help us to keep a light hold of the false self and to let it go more easily. With humour the true Self emerges and we establish an atmosphere of gentleness, harmony, acceptance, forgiveness, patience and compassion. The atmosphere of safety and belonging is deepened.

In conclusion, healing and resolving our childhood wounds involves recognising our emotional needs and fear-based feelings (the topic of chapter 6). It brings to our conscious awareness the childhood dramas we always re-enact, particularly in the classroom environment, which places high demands on the professional conduct of teachers. When we are under stress, we do not always have conscious control over our thoughts and emotions. Therefore, we react in irrational ways when the wounding buttons are pushed. The way out is to take good care of ourselves (the topic explored in chapter 6).

> *It is when we start understanding the cause and effect relationship between what happened to the child we were, and the effect it had on the adult we became, that we can truly start to forgive ourselves. It is only when we start understanding on an emotional level, on a gut level, that we were powerless to do any differently than we did, that we can truly start to love ourselves.*
> *(Robert Burney)*

▶ Taking action!

Three suggestions for putting the ideas in this chapter into practice:

1. Review the self-assessment of your development needs. Identify those needs that were not adequately fulfilled. Find ways to fulfill them as an adult. What can you do to provide for the needs of your inner child?

2. Catch negative thoughts about yourself. These are most probably the voice of your inner critic. Quieten your mind and reassure the inner critic that all is well. Explore the positive, well-meaning intentions of your inner critic and negotiate alternative behaviours.

3. Reflect on classroom incidents where you have lost your cool. What triggered your emotional outburst? Which predominant feelings emerged: anger, shame, guilt or fear? How did you deal with your reaction? Identify the childhood wound, and if possible, embrace it and love it. Then try and let it go.

Review questions

1. Describe the nurturance needs of children and the effects of emotional and spiritual deprivation.
2. How do the messages children receive from parents, teachers and caregivers affect them?
3. Explain the link between the false self and the true Self.
4. What is the role of the inner critic? How can adults deal with the voice of the inner critic?
5. Describe the characteristics of Grown Wounded Children and the recovery process.
6. Why is it important for teachers to be conscious of the phenomenon of Grown Wounded Children?

✓ In a snapshot

1. Children internalise the messages they receive from adults. Negative messages have a disempowering effect as they lower the child's self-esteem.
2. Children adopt a false self to protect their true Self. The false self unconsciously dominates adult behaviour. It influences the potential to form healthy connections with others. Therefore, conscious recovery from childhood emotional wounds is important.
3. Grown Wounded Children are adults who survived unintended emotional and spiritual deprivation imposed by their early childhood caregivers, parents and teachers.
4. Teachers should be aware of how unresolved wounded child emotions affect their interaction with learners.

Suggested reading

Branden, N. (1994) *Six Pillars of Self-esteem*. New York: Bantam

Burney, R. (2006) Loving the Wounded Child Within. Retrieved from the World Wide Web on 23 January 2006, http://www.joy2meu.com//innerchild.html

Elias, MJ. (2001) 'Easing transitions with social-emotional learning' *Principal Leadership*, 1(7): 20–25

Epstein, R. (2000) *The Big Book of Stress Relief Games*. New York: McGraw-Hill

Ferrini, P. (1996) *The Silence of the Heart*. Greenfield, MA: Heartwayspress

Mather, N. & Goldstein, S. (2001) *Learning Disabilities and Challenging Behaviours*. Illinois: Paul H. Brookes Publishing Co

Chapter 6 Be good to yourself

In chapter 5 we discussed the importance of doing inner work to heal our childhood wounds. This chapter takes a closer look at how to deal with stress and how to nurture our emotional needs.

Apart from healing their emotional lives, teachers need to maintain their health and vitality. The school, and in particular, the classroom environment places extreme physical and emotional demands upon teachers. Emotional intelligence enables teachers to manage stress, to take care of themselves and to be good to themselves. It opens up space for teachers use their energy more efficiently and to maintain their health and sense of well-being in the midst of everyday pressures.

When you recognise that your emotions, as well as others', can be capricious at times, you are better able to forgive and forget. (Deepak Chopra)

What is stress?

Stress is an adaptive response to the experience of unpleasant over- or under-stimulation. If not managed, stress actually or potentially leads to ill health. Daily stimulation and challenge are part of life. They provide excitement, impetus and motivation. However, they also cause distress and anxiety. As long as we feel in control, challenge can be invigorating. The challenges that teachers face in the classroom evoke disabling feelings. Actions associated with stress start to take hold. Stress affects us in four ways:
1. *Physically*, causing headaches, stomach upsets, fatigue, frequent colds or flu, asthma or wheezing, poor sleep, muscle tension, nausea, too little or too much eating.
2. *Mentally*, impairing logical thinking.
3. *Emotionally*, creating tension, irritability and frequent feelings of anxiety, sadness, frustration or anger.
4. *Behaviourally*, by affecting the way we act, for example, the typical behavioural patterns of thinking or feeling types.

In times of stress, the nervous system triggers the release of the stress hormones: adrenalin, norepinephrine and cortisol. These hormones stimulate every system in the body during the stress response and start up a range of bodily reactions. For example, they cause sugars and fats to pour into the bloodstream for quick energy. The blood pressure rises and the heart beats faster to boost circulation to muscles in the arms and legs. Respiration increases to supply more oxygen. The blood clots more easily as a precaution against injury. Perspiration increases to cool the body in its energised state.

The stress response happens very quickly. It is designed to save our lives in case of emergency. Once danger is past, the body gradually returns to its normal state. Most of the time, we do not experience stress as a physical threat. Rather, we meet it as time pressure, noisy or resistant learners in the classroom, heavy traffic or the weight of responsibility. However, the effects on the body, mind and emotions are profound.

No matter how much stress you experience, and regardless of the physical or emotional toll it exacts, you can do something about it. Emotional intelligence skills identify the causes of stress and enable us to recognise the danger signs. This seven-step action plan outlines the skills needed to respond to stress meaningfully:

1. Identify your stress triggers.
2. Recognise your emotional needs.
3. Listen to your body.
4. Practise the calm response.
5. Balance your emotions.
6. Accept what you cannot change.
7. Practise a lower stress life.

Step 1 Identify your stress triggers

Identify the difference between self-nurturance and addiction. Many individuals engage in addictive behaviours or take addictive substances to cover up emotions they cannot handle. (Christiane Northrup)

Stress is the result of a mismatch between the challenges we experience and our belief in our ability to cope. Challenges may come from external sources, for example, learner behaviour in the classroom, busy schedules or heavy traffic. Stress may even be the result of too much or too little pressure. These challenges arise from within us. They are the product of our personality preferences (thinking or feeling type), value systems, unfulfilled emotional needs and expectations.

Feeling uncomfortable with or overwhelmed by your workload is a red flag to stress. Not only does it mean that your physical and emotional resilience is being sapped; it also means that you are not taking responsibility for getting the help you need.

We cannot control stress if we are not sure of what lies behind it. The causes of stress must be identified at their first signs. Once we can identify our stress triggers and consider solutions, we start feeling a sense of control that we did not have before. Feeling in control of our lives is one of the best ways to combat stress, which is what emotional intelligence is all about.

It is not uncommon for teachers to feel so tired and burnt-out that they cannot begin to muster the energy required for problem-solving. At that point, it makes sense to see a therapist right away. A professional therapist helps us to learn more about ourselves and points out practical ways to bring calm into our lives.

> **Try this now!**
>
> 1. Review the characteristics of your personality preference (thinking or feeling type). Write down the stress triggers for your type.
>
>   **My personality preference**
>
>   **Typical stress triggers**
>
> 2. Sit down for a few minutes every day to write about issues that concern you. Do not waste time writing about the little things, like driving in traffic. Rather, try to get to the source of what is bothering you, for example, feeling unappreciated. At that point, you can start problem-solving. Make a list of some of your options, for example, talk to a counsellor or express your needs.
>
>   **Issues that concern me**
>
>   **What is really bothering me?**
>
>   **My options**

Step 2 Recognise your emotional needs

The feelings we experience are largely the result of our emotional needs. Unmet emotional needs lead to negative, fear-based feelings. We feel we do not receive what we strive for. We are frustrated, unfulfilled and unhappy. These feelings lead to stress, and when prolonged, to burn-out and depression.

Our worries, concerns and fear-based feelings when our emotional needs are not fulfilled cause limbic stress. This is the pressure and inner distress that arises from out-of-control negative emotions created in the brain by the limbic system. The anger, worry, hurts or fears seem like a repetitive cycle, a broken CD, that destroys our inner calm and happiness. Negative emotions degrade our quality of life. They create distress long after the actual stressing event has passed.

We carry these negative emotions into the classroom and they have a negative impact on the learning and teaching atmosphere. Fears are worries taken to the extreme. The secret is to keep them from getting blown out of proportion. Distress continues until we comfort the roots of anger, worry, hurt or fear through a soothing comforting connection. Table 6.1 identifies the comforting connections for your emotional needs.

Your primary comforting connection is to have a plan. You want to feel prepared, in control and not vulnerable.

Try this now!

Find your comforting connection

Use these two strategies to comfort yourself during worry, hurt, anger or fear:

1. Right now, what would comfort me in this situation? What in essence would soothe me?
2. How can I give that essence or sensation to myself? What action can I take? What can I focus on mentally to create a positive feeling in my body?

Table 6.1 Suggestions for comforting connections

Emotion	Comforting connection
Rejection Fully accept, do not reject yourself.	You want to feel accepted. How can you give acceptance to yourself? What action or self-praise emphasises how much you value yourself?
Betrayal Do not feel helpless.	You want to feel less helpless, like a victim. Focus on the positive action you can take. Do not be unfair to yourself by feeling that you allowed the betrayal. Forgive yourself and let go.
Loneliness Want to feel part of a greater whole.	You do not want to feel alone. Find ways to feel and cherish your connection to the Universe, to all of life. Enjoy being part of the groups in your life, such as your learners.
Loss of loved ones Soul-cherish your memories.	You want to feel them in your life. Remember that every event is still happening somewhere in space time. You can travel to your memories and relive them, cherishing rather than missing your loved ones.
Loss of job/opportunity Focus on a new beginning and learning.	You want to feel in control and valued. Focus on what you have learned from the situation, and/or how it has made you stronger. Emphasise your opportunity for a new beginning.
Not feeling loved/appreciated Remember to love/appreciate yourself unconditionally.	You want to feel loved and appreciated. Remember that the most crucial love is your love of self. Focus on loving and/or cherishing yourself, e.g. self-praise, taking yourself on a date or to a movie, giving yourself time off, or a special treat.
Not feeling heard Write or say what you want to be heard about.	You want to feel heard. Identify exactly what the issue is, as well as how and when to communicate it.
Anger at self Allow yourself to learn.	You want to feel less disappointed in yourself. Focus on perfecting yourself rather than having to be perfect.

Feeling helpless Emphasise what you can do.	You want to feel less helpless. Look for anything that you can do. It focuses your attention on how to take greater command of your life.
Feeling controlled Realise you can always control your attitude.	You want to feel less controlled. Remember that even in the most restrictive circumstances, you can still be in control of your own happiness. You may not be able to change the situation, but you can control your state of mind.
Not being valued Find a way to value/cherish yourself.	You want to feel valued. Make sure you value yourself fully. Acknowledge and praise yourself rather than looking to others for your own worth.
Irritation/anger Put it into perspective and control your attitude.	You want to feel less hassled and more at ease. Do not let little irritations win and take control of your inner environment. Watch out for food and stimulants like caffeine that cause a hormonal imbalance in your body.
Feeling responsible Be response-able, making choices versus focusing on pressure.	You want to feel you can handle it. Remember that you choose how to respond to situations. If necessary, make a plan that outlines your choices for any "what if" situation. Then acknowledge that you can choose from that list when the time arises.
Financial Make a plan of how to stretch your resources.	You want to feel more secure. Outline your options and find ways to know what is possible and what is not.
Job security Plan your options and prepare for them.	You want to feel less uncertain. Look into other options and prepare your resume. Go for job training so that you feel prepared.
About family/learners Remember they are learning souls too.	You want to feel less helpless. Remember that they, as souls, must live their own life purposes and that there are forces to help and guide them. Remember to care about them, but not worry for them.

Step 3 Listen to your body

Our emotions, like our bodies, provide us with a considerable amount of information. Minor aches and pains, body temperature and illness tell us a number of things about what we are truly feeling.

In reviewing your emotional intelligence profile, it is important to consider your relationship with your body. How do you treat it? How do you feel about it? Do you get enough exercise? Do you follow a healthy, energising diet? If you treat your body well, you will respect yourself more. You will have the energy you need to manage stressful events and everyday pressure.

> **! Try this now!**
>
> Take a moment to pay attention to your body. Which parts of your body come spontaneously to your awareness? Which parts do you have difficulty contacting? Notice the pressure, movement, energy and tension you feel. Deliberately exaggerate any sensations if you want to be aware of them. What kind of message does this sensation give you?

Step 4 Practise the calm response

The physical symptoms of stress can make life uncomfortable. There are six ways to control the symptoms of stress and bring calm into your life.

1. *Breathe deeply.* Experts agree that shallow, chest breathing is associated with anxiety, high blood pressure, nervous disorders, depression and psychosomatic disorders. Deep breathing, using the diaphragm muscle and belly, quietens the mind. It reduces blood pressure, uplifts unhealthy attitudes, calms the emotions and decreases psychosomatic symptoms.
2. *Get some sun.* Even if you do not think you have the time, go outside for a few minutes. Exposure to sunlight increases levels of serotonin, a natural hormone that reduces stress and imparts a feeling of calm and well-being.
3. *Take mini-breaks.* Let your mind rest for at least five minutes every hour and you will find it easier to stay calm and focused. Close your eyes and think peaceful thoughts. Stand up and stretch, or better still, walk briskly for a few moments to release endorphins, the body chemicals that neutralise the stress hormones.
4. *Distract yourself.* Fill your free time with the activities you love, for example, gardening, hiking or painting. They will help keep your mind off the stress of tomorrow.
5. *Rewrite the script.* If you believe that an unruly class of learners is a catastrophe, then take a new perspective. Instead of losing it, try and see the humour. Turn life into a comedy instead of a drama.
6. *Remember the anchors in your life.* When things feel like they are spinning out of control, take an inventory of all the things you know that are solid and reliable. For example, your child is safe; you have food in your home and a roof over your head; your car will get you to work on time; you have the support and love of your family or a close friend; you have employment. When we realise how much in our lives is dependable, we have more trust in our ability to work through life's problems.

If you don't move your body, your brain thinks you're dead. Movement of the body will not only clear out the sludge, but will also give you more energy. Treat your body like a car – keep it tuned up and it will run for a very long time.
(Sylvia Browne)

> **! Try this now!**
>
> **Make me laugh.**
>
> Humour can be used to reinterpret what is happening or to defuse a tense situation.
>
> Write down three stressful situations, for example, dysfunctional behaviour in class, conflict with a colleague, some problem with a learner's performance, or a tight deadline. Explore ways in which humour might be used to improve the situation.

Step 5 Balance your emotions

Accept all your emotions, the good and the bad. Allow yourself to experience all of your feelings, including negative emotions, such as hostility or anger. Know and understand that you can choose which behaviour you will use to response to negative emotions.

Move beyond negative thoughts. Everyone is self-critical at times. Pay attention to how you criticise yourself. Expose these thoughts to a more rational evaluation. Write them down or tell them to a friend. It is important to act in your own self-interest, rather than on negative self-critical thoughts.

> **! Try this now!**
>
> Make a list of the activities and people that bring you joy. Then make a list of those that bring negative emotions. Look at the lists every day. Do whatever you can to embrace the good and avoid the bad. Find ways to see them in a new light and to transform the bad into good.
>
> **Activities that bring me joy**
>
> **People who bring me joy**
>
> **Activities that bring negative emotions**
>
> **People who bring negative emotions**

Step 6 Accept what you cannot change

Stress will never go away. Teachers have to accept that. However, it is important to remember that stress is not the issue. What is at stake is the way we react to it. No matter what life throws at you, find a way to unwind, for example:
1. *Accept the circumstances.* You cannot resolve some types of stress. Breathing and relaxation help, but nothing will take

away the heartache or the grief over the death of someone you felt close to. Stay in touch with your sense of loss or pain. Give yourself time to work through the emotion and be kind to yourself.
2. *Be imperfect and calmer.* Teachers who try to achieve the unachievable feel frustrated, anxious or depressed. Concentrate on your strengths, instead of obsessing over your flaws. The moment a negative thought enters your mind, replace it by saying, "I'm doing the best I can."
3. *Acknowledge your mistakes and move on.* Because so many people depend on teachers, they feel as though they have to make the right decisions every time. It does not work that way. Accept that everyone makes mistakes. Do not dwell on them. Forgive yourself. Let go and move on.

> **! Try this now!**
>
> Forgiveness is fundamental to our sense of well-being. If you hold things against yourself or others, you end up punishing yourself in many ways including not allowing yourself to succeed.
>
> 1. *Identify* the things that you want to forgive yourself for. Be as specific as possible. Think of behaviour, feelings, thoughts, habits and addictions.
> 2. *Own your responsibility* for the situation. Be honest with yourself. Feel the regret, the remorse or the sorrow for the negative impact.
> 3. *Release* the pain and release the past. Allow yourself to release them.
> 4. *Forgive* yourself. Forgive anyone else.

Step 7 Practise a lower stress life

We can establish three very good habits every day, even when we are not under stress, to make us a little calmer when things go awry:

Habit 1 Exercise regularly. It is one of the best ways to reduce anxiety, tension, apprehension, depression and fatigue. Physical activity releases feel good endorphins which help us to calm down and relax.

Habit 2 Get a pet. Studies have shown that a cat, a dog or any other pet reduces stress.

Habit 3 Energise your life. Think positively about the coming day when you rise in the morning. Find a reason to get out of bed. Take care of and be disciplined in your eating habits. Listen to the wisdom of your body.

Eat stress-free food

What we eat has a direct influence on our moods, energy levels, thinking processes, sleeping habits and stress levels. Get into the habit of reading food labels, so that you know which products to use and which ones to avoid. The food we eat and drink are the building blocks of the neurotransmitters involved in brain activity. Peptides, steroids, serotonin, dopamine, norepinephrine and acetylcholine are especially important.

Avoid stimulants such as caffeine in coffee, chocolate, cola, tea, diet drugs and some pain relievers. They increase levels of fatigue and irritability. Drink plenty pure water, at least eight glasses a day. Water makes up three quarters of the human body. Brain tissue consists of over 80 percent water. After water, the best fluids are fruit and vegetable juices, natural mineral water and most herbal teas. These thin the blood, flush out toxins and prevent the body from being poisoned by its own waste matter.

Choose complex carbohydrates, such as whole grains, pulses and other plant foods. They are broken down slowly during digestion and produce and release glucose (blood sugar) at a steady pace, thus maintaining energy levels.

Avoid simple carbohydrates, such as sweet snacks and drinks. They cause blood sugar levels to rise and the body responds by releasing overly large amounts of insulin. This can make you feel tired and even depressed. In addition, if you overdo it, too much insulin can cause lack of concentration, mood swings and irritability.

The secret of managing stress is to balance the variety of methods available. An overreliance on and overuse of any one method can cause more problems than it solves. For example, sleeping pills or alcohol help us to relax and may be valuable on occasion. However, daily use leads to sluggishness and addiction.

Thinking types who tend to rely too much on tackling problems head on, but do not allow themselves to express their feelings must guard that they do not become exhausted and emotionally distant, even from the people to whom they are closest.

Feeling types who tend to neglect nurturing themselves, but are experts at distracting themselves by helping other people, must see that they do not become drained and overwhelmed by the endless demands made on them.

> **! Try this now!**
>
> **How balanced is your stress toolkit?**
> Make a list of the ways in which you have dealt with stress to date. Include the ordinary, everyday methods. Delete those which you consider to be negative, and which result in more stress. Look at the strategies described in this book and add to your list the ones which apply to you. Categorise the methods under the headings below.
>
> **Problem-solving**
>
> **Active distraction** (e.g. hobbies, taking a walk)
>
> **Self-nurturing** (e.g. rest, relaxation, diet, having a massage)
>
> **Emotional expression** (e.g. expressing feelings verbally to a friend; creative emotional expression by writing poetry or painting; catharsis, having a good cry or screaming without hurting anyone)

Once you have learned to balance the different strategies and habits of stress management, you will raise your energy level, develop your potential to take on more responsibility, use the talents you may not yet be aware of, improve your relationships with learners, colleagues and at home, and initiate changes to succeed in achieving your goals in life.

> **! Try this now!**
>
> **Create a nirvana room**
> (*Nirvana: the Buddhist state of perfect bliss and peacefulness*)
> The best classroom effuses a sense of calm, while keeping productivity high. Carefully study these five principles:
>
> 1. The *irritation principle*: Stimuli that irritate the senses can cause stress, for example, loud noises, echoes, clashing colours, broken windows, untidiness.
> 2. The *soothing principle*: Stimuli that soothe the senses can relieve stress, for example, soft music, dim lighting, tidiness, garden scents, flowers, plants.
> 3. The *overstimulation principle*: Overstimulation can cause stress, for example, several learners speaking simultaneously, the sound of many machines operating.
> 4. The *minimal principle*: Low stimulation can relieve stress, for example, a quiet, harmonious environment, discipline and order in the classroom, a walk in nature, sitting in the shade of a tree.
> 5. The *colourful principle*: A soothing colour scheme can relieve stress, for example, low-saturation colours, cool colours (in the blue-green range). Rose pink engenders friendship and generally brings people together. Bright yellow enhances concentration and stimulates productivity. Pale blue calms angry situations. Bright green brings a sense of aliveness. Bright orange and red activate restlessness.
>
> Which of these principles have you already applied in your classroom. What changes, large and small, can be created in your classroom relax both you and your learners? Involve your learners in this exercise and let them share their ideas with you. Keep individual differences in mind. What is irritating to one person might be soothing to another.

Releasing suppressed emotions

Negative emotions frequently result in physical symptoms. It is normal, for example, for us to feel tired or lethargic before we actually identify the underlying emotion, such as anger or rage. When for apparently no good reason you are physically off-colour, it is likely that your emotions are out of balance and that you are suppressing a core emotion, such as anger, shame, guilt, sadness or fear.

There are some emotions that we do not feel comfortable with, for example, anger or jealousy. However, these feelings will come out at some time or another. Unexpressed emotions are toxic to us and our bodies. They pollute our emotional life, our relationships, and in time, our bodies. Unexpressed hurt or fear, for example, can present in the body as aches and pains.

Dr John Bell (2003) writes that we are all meant to have a rich emotional life and to think and feel in depth. The only negative emotion is one that is suppressed. Ideally, we should be able to allow for the natural flow of thoughts and feelings, and feel and express all our emotions in a socially responsible (emotionally intelligent) manner.

Unfortunately, many people in western culture are taught from an early age to suppress or repress their emotions. This long-term suppression means that they are no longer capable of contacting certain emotions. They unable to express or release them. For example, research indicates that western women tend to lose touch with their ability to express anger, while men tend to suppress fear or grief.

If such suppression is allowed to continue, it eventually emerges in the form of physical or mental illness, for example, depression. Learning how to manage our stress and how to release blocked feelings so as to recover the ability to express the full range of our emotions increases our vitality and creativity.

Consciously developing and using emotional intelligence skills helps to reconnect with our long-term suppressed emotions which are linked to wounded child issues (see chapter 5).

In chapter 2 we took a closer look at core emotions that influence our health and sense of well-being. Let's review some of the most important emotions that we all tend to suppress.

Anger

Anger is an active emotion. If not expressed appropriately, in time it will process itself out through the body and creates ill health. We can learn to express our anger honestly and cleanly, and to release it properly.

Rather than push anger away, work out what it is telling you. Say to yourself, "I am angry because something is wrong." This will help you work out what needs fixing.

Feeling the emotion is not the same as acting on it. If you are boiling with rage, ask yourself whether the present moment is the right time and place to express it. You may prefer to go to a private place to vent it, or to take a long walk to think things over.

There is nothing wrong with confronting people who have made you angry. However, you must wait until you cool off. Then explain to them how their words or actions made you feel. As long as you approach people calmly and with a genuine desire to work things out, they will co-operate with you to find a solution.

Shame

Shame (low self-esteem/self disdain) is the primal emotion related to believing "I am a worthless, unlovable, disgusting, inept, stupid, ugly person/male/female." This crippling belief starts in early childhood, if we are taught that our worth depends on pleasing other people, for example, parents and teachers. Scorn, exclusion and disrespect promote local or enduring shame. This shame promotes self-neglect and addiction. Low nurturance environments, such as an emotionally cold classroom can create feelings of excessive shame.

Some parents and teachers use humiliation and shame as a way of controlling children. As children, we were too young to deal with this emotion and so we learned to suppress it. Eventually shame becomes a state of being, and not just something we feel. We truly believe we are unworthy, disgusting and useless.

Shame is the seedbed for addictions, both negative ones like substance abuse or sexual promiscuity, and the positive ones like work and goodness, for example, always being nice. We compensate for our defectiveness by trying to be perfect or superhuman. Dr John Bell (2003) writes that shame eventually becomes a gaping wound or a hole that can never be filled.

Unresolved shame can cause us to give up on ourselves on life. Ultimately, we need to find the courage to own our shame, to look at how it has polluted our lives and our relationships. We need to allow ourselves to grieve the losses it has caused us and then release it and heal it.

Many adults pass their own unresolved shame on to the next generation. Teachers who are not self-aware, may unconsciously dump their suppressed shame onto learners. Their undealt with shame may be acted out as rage and pain in their interactions with learners. They project their denied shame onto learners, and see them as disgusting. They verbally humiliate learners in front of their peers. Such teachers only set themselves up for more rejection. They are abandoned and betrayed by their learners who could lose respect for the teacher. This rejection has a cyclical effect; it confirms what the teacher subconsciously believes, that he or is is really tainted and worthless.

Because teachers are role models to learners, it is critical for them, as adults, to heal and release their feelings of shame. Shame is complex and it takes professional assistance from a therapist or counsellor for healing to set in.

Shame can be handled positively by feeling deep *remorse* for our actions and behaviour towards others. Remorse helps us to forgive ourselves. Remorse allows us to make mistakes. Shame, on the other hand, equates making a mistake with being a mistake. In a dysfunctional family or classroom, many parents and teachers think that the behaviour of their children and learners reflects on them. Not wanting to feel ashamed, they make the children and learners feel ashamed instead.

As teachers the onus is on us to own and heal the wounds of the past so that we can truly live in the present. Once healed, we are less likely to pass on the wounds to the next generation. We need to discover our innate value, our true Self, so that we do not perpetuate a distorted value system, and so that we can truly love and allow ourselves to be loved.

Fear and anxiety

The emotion of fear was discussed in chapter 2. Fear indicates a limiting belief. Too much fear can overwhelm us, so we cannot think clearly or make the right decisions. The ultimate fear is fear of rejection, abandonment and loneliness.

Excessive feelings of fear result in anxiety and worry. When we feel anxious or worried it is important to identify the underlying emotion of hurt, anger or fear.

> **! Try this now!**
>
> Anxiety can cause panic attacks, a racing heart, nausea, chest pain, dizziness and other symptoms. To combat this:
>
> 1. *Take a deep breath*: Deep breathing is a good way to reduce shortness of breath, a racing heart or other anxiety symptoms.
> 2. *Stop irrational thoughts*: Anxiety is caused by catastrophic thinking, that is, the belief that the worst is about to happen. Mentally shout, "Stop!" At the same time, distract yourself, for example, count backwards from 100. Your mind will find it difficult to return to the same troublesome thoughts.

True courage is the ability to take positive action in spite of the fear. (John Bell)

Fear must be confronted, rather than denied. Therefore, find and change any faulty belief lurking behind fear. Fear disguises our emotional needs. Understanding our true emotional needs will lead us to tap into our comforting connections (see table 6.1) and successfully release suppressed fear from our bodies.

To release our fear we must have the courage to let in the emotion of love. Allowing love into our lives, and experiencing it fully, releases feelings of fear. Love is the positive emotion from which all other positive emotions, such as peace, joy, happiness, and enthusiasm, flow. Unfortunately many people fear the vulnerability that love brings. The more we love, the greater our fear of loss or being hurt. Some people also fear being perceived as too joyful, in case others regard them as being simple-minded.

> **! Try this now!**
>
> Take a few moments to relax. Go and stand in the sun. Breathe deeply, close your eyes and feel the warm rays of the sun caressing your skin. Open your arms and welcome the nurturing warmth that the sun provides. Feel the love that it brings.
>
> Allow yourself to feel the love that you have for the sun, the earth, life, your true Self and for others.
>
> Allow yourself to feel all the love that family and friends have for you. Stand in that love, open your heart to receive it. Know that you are worthy. Feel and receive the love fully. You deserve it.

Hurt and guilt

Unlike anger that flares up and quickly subsides, *hurt* wounds us and takes time to heal. Intentionally hurting others causes distress and pain. It is not socially acceptable behaviour. Hurtful behaviour towards others leads to guilt. Guilt is the normal emotional reaction to the protective inner critic proclaiming, "You broke a rule, a should (not), must (not), or ought (not). Therefore, you did something wrong."

Some people use the excuse of being hurt as a way of manipulating others. If someone makes you feel guilty, beneath the guilt you are bound to find anger. Physical pain or discomfort reflects the buried emotional pain of being hurt. Guilt amplifies personal shame and feels similar to it. Moderate shame and guilt (remorse) promote healthy personal decisions. A good way to come to terms with guilt and to shrink it to a manageable size is to discuss your feelings with others, be it a friend, family member or therapist. The guilt and shame looming large in your own mind will appear small to other people. This will help you to put your feelings into perspective.

> **! Try this now!**
>
> **It's time to stop pretending you are small.**
>
> Thoughts give birth to emotions. First, there is the thought and then the emotion arises. Any emotion created by entirely the false self is limited because you are using the limitations of the false self (the inner critic) to create it. Thus the most horrendous feeling, fantasy or fear has a limit to it. You can get rid of anything that is limited. Emotions like fear, anger, grief or judgement can be removed if you so desire.
>
> See in your mind's eye a 100 000 kilometer tsunami-like wave coming towards you. Most probably your response is, "Get me out of here!" That is how you feel in the face of strong emotions. The small, frightened, childlike part of you responds like this because life looked so overwhelming when you were little. But it does not have to be like that. You are not little. You are vast. Your true Self contains untapped power and potential to be all that you can be. It is time to stop pretending you are small. Stop pretending you are afraid. Stop pretending and become aware of what is happening by staying with your fears. Experience them fully. Do not run. Remember you are vast, with infinite resources. You have the capability to overcome whatever you want and need to. You are not the victim of your life.
>
> You are the 100 000 kilometer wave, as well as those feelings of being two centimetres high. Your true Self, your real strength, your reservoir of potential possibility, change and extension is a 100 000 kilometer wave. This fearful feeling or remembrance of a past event that is not even here anymore is just a fragment drifting in and out of the vastness. The fragment comes and goes. It is not permanent. As you watch this coming and going, this drifting of negative emotions, you will experience directly that you yourself are not that fear. Fear is something that enters you and then exists. So pay close attention. This is where you will learn control over your own thoughts and emotions.
>
> Concentrate on what you wish to have in your life. What you concentrate on, you make real, you make present. If you are flooded with difficult feelings, you now know you yourself can create expansive, love-based feelings. It is your reluctance to let go of the negativity that keeps you trapped. Drop negativity from your mind. Realise you are creating it; you are doing this to yourself. Your past cannot trap you unless you allow it. Drop the past and be here now. Learn the delight and joy of just stepping out into a different feeling frequency. Let your emotions work for you. Step into something else. Leave the past behind. Choose to step into peace, into joy, into compassion and enter something new and different. From that new and different place, quietly allow the past to dissolve. Welcome to happiness.
>
> *(Based on Bartholomew, 1999)*

Feelings form the basis of our relations with learners. They are the key to creating a high nurturance, emotionally warm classroom environment. By allowing ourselves to think and feel and then to reflect, we grow in self-awareness, self-understanding, and most importantly, we regain our sense of aliveness and joy for life.

By respecting our emotional nature, we reconnect with our true Self. Our courage to let go of the false self, increases as we regain self-respect and truly acknowledge our worth. The challenge is to take the first step and to release the emotional crutches we have carried with us all our life. It is time to give our lives wings, to be free. If not now, then when?

▶ Taking action!

Four suggestions to put the ideas in this chapter into practice:

1. *Identify your stress triggers.* Evaluate your stress toolkit and add strategies that may help you towards a more balanced approach to manage your stress.

2. *Make a list – even if it is painful – of emotions you have suppressed for a long time.* Study the strategies to release these emotions. Revisit chapter 2 for additional guidance. Challenge yourself to take the first step today.

3. *Evaluate your overall lifestyle.* Observe your sleeping patterns, exercise, diet, attitudes, thoughts, feelings about life and your learners. Identify which of those habits energise you and which ones drain you. Make a commitment today to deal with unhealthy habits. Do it, because you are worth it.

4. *Identify your emotional needs and comforting connections.* Write down the life issue or fear that is bothering you. Ask yourself what would comfort you in the particular situation. Identify the essence of what you want. What action can you take? What can focus on mentally to create positive healing in your body?

Review questions

1. How does stress affect us and what are the implications for teachers?
2. What triggers stress? Suggest strategies for dealing effectively with stress.
3. Why is it important to recognise and release suppressed emotions?
4. Suggest ways to release suppressed emotions.

✓ In a snapshot

1. Apart from healing their emotional lives, teachers need to be skillful in maintaining their health and vitality. The school, and in particular, the classroom environment, places extreme physical and emotional demands upon teachers. Emotional intelligence includes our ability to manage stress.

2. Stress affects us in four ways: physically, mentally, emotionally and behaviourally. There are a variety of methods to balance and manage our stress effectively.

3. Our emotional needs and suppressed emotions cause stress. Finding the right comforting connection to fullfil our emotional needs and releasing repressed emotions are critical for health and general well-being.

Suggested reading

Branden, N. (1994) *Six Pillars of Self-esteem*. New York: Bantam

Elias, MJ. (2001) 'Easing transitions with social-emotional learning' *Principal Leadership*, 1 (7): 20–25

Epstein, R. (2000) *The Big Book of Stress Relief Games*. New York: McGraw-Hill

Hay, LL. (2004) *Everyday Positive Thinking*. Johannesburg: Hay House

Mulligan, J. (1988) *The Personal Management Handbook: How to Make the Most of Your Potential*. London: Guild Publishing

Preston, DL. (2005) *365 Ways To Be Your Own Life Coach*. Oxford: Howtobooks

Prevention (editors) (2004) *The Women's Health Bible*. London: Rodale

Chapter 7　Do it ... because you can!

This chapter recommends steps for you to achieve excellence as a professional educator. By understanding the power of managing your emotions and thought patterns, you will open the door to a new awareness.

As you model the things that emotionally intelligent teachers believe and do, you will introduce a whole new world of satisfying experiences to the classroom. Consciously practising and applying the principles of emotional intelligence will make a big difference in your life.

This chapter is for teachers who want to reach a deeper level of understanding whereby they flow easily and effectively in interactions with their learners. The recommendations simply reflect the truths that successful teachers have learned by working consciously with the principles underlying emotionally intelligent behaviour. Such teachers know deep down in their hearts that the seven aspects of their emotional intelligence gives them freedom and the edge over others. These are:

1. Motivation;
2. Clarity about the six conditions of emotional creativity in the classroom;
3. Understanding of the impact of behavioural preferences;
4. The ability to monitor the classroom emotional climate;
5. Recognition of the blocks and the ability to stop destructive patterns immediately;
6. Using flexibility to their advantage; and
7. The Ten Day Plan to Excellence to create a positive emotional climate in the classroom.

Let go of small thoughts about yourself! See yourself succeeding. (Doreen Virtue)

To keep progressing, you must learn, commit and do – learn, commit and do – and learn, commit and do all over again! (Stephen R. Covey)

Happy and successful teachers are motivated to use their emotional intelligence in creating classroom conditions that foster their learners' performance and growth. This is an important part of their life's purpose because they have a passion for their teaching subject and they enjoy sharing their wisdom and knowledge.

Getting motivated

There are different ways to get motivated. We all have a motivation direction: this direction is either *towards* what we want or *away from* what we do not want. The motivation direction is a mental programme that affects our entire lives.

At the biological or physical level, we have developed both away from and towards motivation. We veer away from pain, discomfort and stress; we move towards pleasure, comfort and relaxation. There are dangerous places, hurtful actions and negative thinking worth moving away from, just as there are wonderful places, supportive, encouraging people and positive thinking worth moving towards.

To some degree we all use both motivation directions. Yet, each one of us gives preference to one direction over the other. We are motivated either towards images of success, pleasure and gains; or away from failure, pain and loss.

At first glance, a side-by-side comparison of the *towards* and *away from* motivation strategies make towards motivation look considerably more appealing. People with a towards motivation are likely to say, "There's a better way to live or teach. Just imagine what you want and go towards it." However, consider what happens when the room temperature is uncomfortable: you do something to change it. Similarly, when a learner behaves badly, you do something about it. These are examples of a positive away from motivation strategy in action.

If you are blessed with a successful and abundant life, one of the things that got you there was most likely the memory of poverty in which you grew up. If remembering those hard times in the past motivates you to keep striving for a better quality of life now, then you have made an appropriate use of your away from motivation.

The benefits of *towards* motivation are more obvious. Our society values people who move towards goals and rewards. When we examine the advantages of both directions, we find that towards motivation is goal oriented and away from motivation is driven by identifying and solving problems.

Both types of motivation have advantages and disadvantages, moderations and extremes. For example, people who are so motivated towards their goals may not consider the problems that could crop up or what difficulties to prepare for along the way. At the other extreme, people who are very away from motivated may be too terrified to try anything new. They focus on solving the problem and forget why they were doing it. While the towards motivation is more commonly appreciated in successful teachers, the less appreciated away from motivation can also lead to success.

> **Try this now!**
>
> **What is your motivation direction?**
> Tick the appropriate motivation. See which ones you have the most of.
>
> | Away from | Towards |
> |---|---|
> | _____ Pain | _____ Pleasure |
> | _____ Discomfort | _____ Comfort |
> | _____ Stress | _____ Relaxation |
> | _____ Failure | _____ Success |
> | _____ Loss | _____ Gain |

Values influence our motivation. At the physical level, motivation direction means moving away from pain and towards pleasure. At the cognitive (thoughts) and emotional (feelings) levels, it means moving away from or towards values. When we become disconnected from our values, we lose our motivation. Successful teachers are deeply connected to values. This helps them to stay motivated and focused on their goals and what they want to achieve.

They live out of their deep values. Deep values lie at the root of all our goals. Knowing our deep values is a crucial aspect of self-understanding. They were the values that motivated us to become teachers, that motivated our achievements, and our every action.

In the classroom context emotional intelligence reveals whether your motivation is based on moving away from a negative classroom atmosphere or towards creating a high nurturance environment to the benefits of all. By honouring your heart-centred values you will develop a towards motivation which energises and allows you to tap into your emotional creativity.

> **Try this now!**
>
> Note your answers to these questions:
>
> - What are my goals?
> - What is important to me?
>
> Your answers could include career achievement, a certain lifestyle, a vacation, or your relationship with your learners. Whatever it is, think of it now. You may even have several goals in mind. Once you have done this, even if some parts are not clear, ask yourself three questions about each goal:
>
> - What is important about this goal?

- What do I value or treasure about this goal?
- What meaning does this goal hold for me?

Your answers to all three questions will give you a list of your deep values. Ask yourself:

- What is important to me about all these values?

The answer that comes to mind will be the most important value for you, your deep values. Once this has been identified, it will be easier for you to stay focused on your intention to display emotional intelligence towards your learners.

Examples of values

aliveness	freedom	learning	simplicity
autonomy	fulfillment	love	solving problems
caring	helping	wisdom	using my abilities
creativity	security	service	making the world a better place

The six conditions of emotional creativity in the classroom

Emotional creativity in the classroom refers to the teacher's ability to foster the conditions that create an emotionally warm classroom climate where children feel motivated and inspired to learn and perform. The six core conditions are depicted in figure 7.1. They are based on the six factors that determine the classroom climate (see chapter 3).

Successful teachers consistently practise and use emotional intelligence to monitor and improve the emotional climate. They know that an optimal teaching and learning environment is not something achieved and fixed. It is fluid and subject to variation through a vast range of dynamic forces acting on the learners. These forces include the learners' socio-emotional needs, their ability, their psychological state, the teacher's overall demeanour and style, and the wider school environment. Classroom conditions can vary from extreme warmth to coldness.

Therefore, managing the classroom climate is difficult because teachers must be sensitive to and understand their learners as individuals and adjust their own behaviour accordingly. Figure 7.1 reflects the behaviour and conditions of the circular and dynamic process of applying emotional creativity to create high nurturance classroom conditions.

Figure 7.1 illustrates how teachers, as secondary educators, are limited in the range of levers available to them in their quest to influence the learners' performance in the broader socio-emotional context of their psychological existence. However, it is evident that the teacher's behavioural sensitivity can and does make a crucial difference in the lives of the learners.

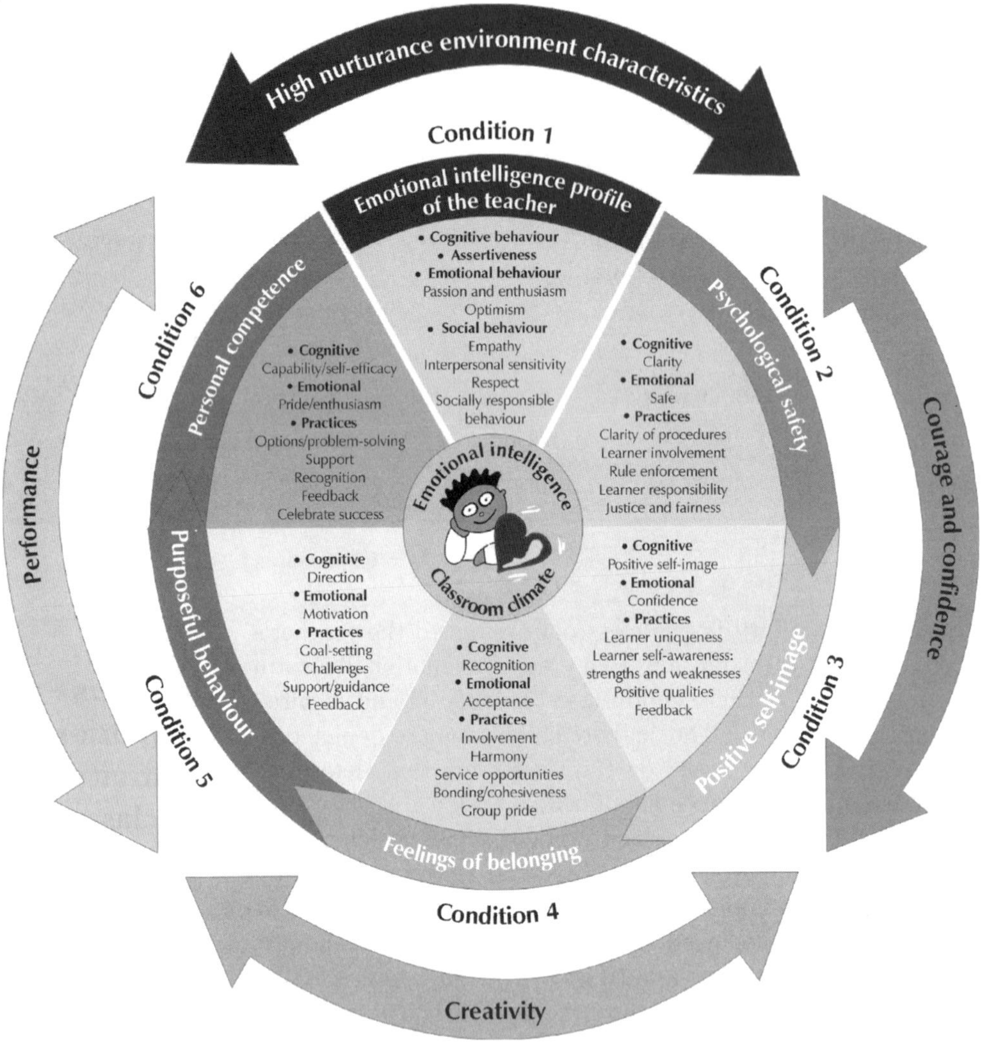
High nurturance environment characteristics
Condition 1
Emotional intelligence profile of the teacher
• Cognitive behaviour
• Assertiveness
• Emotional behaviour
Passion and enthusiasm
Optimism
• Social behaviour
Empathy
Interpersonal sensitivity
Respect
Socially responsible behaviour
Condition 2
Psychological safety
• Cognitive
Clarity
• Emotional
Safe
• Practices
Clarity of procedures
Learner involvement
Rule enforcement
Learner responsibility
Justice and fairness
Courage and confidence
Condition 3
Positive self-image
• Cognitive
Positive self-image
• Emotional
Confidence
• Practices
Learner uniqueness
Learner self-awareness: strengths and weaknesses
Positive qualities
Feedback
Condition 4
Feelings of belonging
• Cognitive
Recognition
• Emotional
Acceptance
• Practices
Involvement
Harmony
Service opportunities
Bonding/cohesiveness
Group pride
Creativity
Condition 5
Purposeful behaviour
• Cognitive
Direction
• Emotional
Motivation
• Practices
Goal-setting
Challenges
Support/guidance
Feedback
Performance
Condition 6
Personal competence
• Cognitive
Capability/self-efficacy
• Emotional
Pride/enthusiasm
• Practices
Options/problem-solving
Support
Recognition
Feedback
Celebrate success
Emotional intelligence
Classroom climate

Figure 7.1 The cycle of emotional creativity in the classroom

Understanding your behavioural preferences

Review how your values (see chapter 3), emotional intelligence and personality preferences (see chapter 4) influence your behavioural patterns in the classroom. Overusing personality preferences (Thinking/Feeling) can make a teacher stuck in specific patterns that create particular classroom conditions. These then become the accepted norm and if they are regarded in a negative light, for example, learners being too afraid to come to class because the teacher is too stern, punitive and unapproachable, then the classroom is labelled as being cold. The teacher may experience the learners' behaviour as resistant. In turn, the teacher could become sterner and more punitive, thus creating a negative cycle.

Negative conditions spawn a spiral of negative attitudes and behaviour. Understanding habitual patterns and consciously developing emotional intelligence will enable you to break these negative cycles. Instead, as shown in figure 7.1, you will create a cycle that reinforces positive learner behaviour.

Emotionally intelligent behaviour opens up emotional creativity that generates positive attitudes and motivated learners. The Ten Day Plan to Excellence offers a way to create a positive cycle that optimises the learners' performance ability.

Table 7.1 Ten secrets of healthier relationships with your learners

1.	*Listen* with the intention of understanding what the learner is saying, feeling, thinking and wanting you to know. Do not interrupt. Do not silently rehearse a reply.
2.	*Understand* and check what the learner has said before you express your own thoughts and feelings. For example, respond with: "You said you thought/ felt/said/did such-and-such. Is this correct?"
3.	*Accept* the learner without accepting his or her beliefs, opinions or behaviour.
4.	*Respect* and believe that the learner is valuable, precious, unique and is doing the best that he or she can at that moment (just like you).
5.	*Empathise* and as far as possible, put yourself in the learner's shoes. Try to really understand where he or she is coming from.
6.	*Be assertive*, but not aggressive. Gently, but firmly express your thoughts.
7.	*Share your feelings*, wants, needs and hopes.
8.	*Speak directly*, but avoid using sarcasm, teasing, belittling, long-winded lectures, withdrawing or sulking. Ask directly for what you want or need.
9.	*Focus on the present* and do not bring up past mistakes or problems.
10.	*Love with unconditional acceptance*: Do unto others as you would have them do unto you.

Monitor the emotional climate

Be alert and daily look out for negative emotional states and destructive behavioural patterns in the classroom. Stop them immediately. Be conscious of your own mood before you enter the classroom. We transfer, even if unconsciously, our own mood and mental-emotional state to the people around us. Similarly, we unconsciously pick up the moods of other people and make them our own. For example, you start the day with a happy and optimistic outlook, but on entering the classroom you realise that your mood has changed and you feel depressed. If we are aware of our own mood, we are more able to distinguish which mood is our own and which moods belong to others.

When you are aware of your own mood and mental-emotional state, you will be able to accurately assess the general atmosphere in the classroom before you start the day. You can then tap into your emotional and intellectual creativity to transform a negative mood into an atmosphere that benefits all. In this way children learn to become aware of their own inner state and how to deal creatively with their emotions and feelings.

Use the Emotional Climate Sensor™[4] on a weekly or bi-weekly basis (or after completing the Ten Day Plan to Excellence) to obtain more accurate information on how well established the core classroom conditions are and how learners perceive the classroom climate. The insights gained will enable you to identify the behaviour and practices that support optimal learning and teaching conditions and those that block the flow of emotional creativity and learning in your classroom.

Recognise the blocks

When teachers monitor and experience the six conditions of the emotional climate in the classroom, they soon learn to identify their own unique behavioural pattern tendencies. The two general patterns are overuse of personality preferences (Thinking/Feeling type) and cyclical correspondences with the six basic classroom conditions (see figure 7.2).

Overusing our personality type (Thinking or Feeling) and acting from our personal value system will lead to our preferred behavioural patterns. Overusing our natural tendencies may steer the classroom towards particular conditions. For example, Thinking types are task-focused and prefer to emphasise purposeful behaviour and competence. However, they overlook the learners' emotional need for feeling that they belong and are accepted as unique beings.

Feeling types, on the other hand, tend to overemphasise the emotional side. They help learners to feel they belong and show empathy, but neglect to set boundaries, exercise discipline, lay down the rules and give the structure that creates psychological safety. They tend not to engage the learners in purposeful behaviour by helping them to set realistic goals and solve their own problems.

An imbalanced use of our decision-making and problem-solving functions leads to an imbalance in the classroom's emotional atmosphere. Fortunately, this is an easy challenge to identify because we only need to recognise that we are repeating

---

[4] The classroom climate can be formally assessed with the *Emotional Climate Sensor*™ developed by and available from the authors.

emotions, behaviours and thoughts over and over again. However, it can prove difficult to overcome because repetition creates incredible intensity and inertia: We become so used to the conditions that we believe that is the way things are. We stop being creative about improving conditions around us.

It is important to distinguish between being stuck in a condition and building upon the processes that create optimal teaching and learning conditions. Happy teachers understand that all conditions must prevail to create a healthy emotional climate in which creativity and performance flourish. Successful teachers know that when we use skills and practices that support us in creating healthy classroom conditions, the experience of satisfaction and happiness outweighs the stress undergone to achieve it.

Table 7.2 Potential development areas

Thinking types	How thinking types benefit from the natural inclination of feeling types
■ Need to consider all sides before deciding, including factoring in the emotional needs of learners. ■ Need to make a special effort to show appreciation of learners. ■ Need to take time to reflect and identify their feelings and values. ■ Need to be sensitive to the general classroom mood and learn to take time to deal with it in constructive ways.	■ Forecast how learners will feel. ■ Pick up the emotional mood of the class and take time to deal with the atmosphere creatively. ■ Praise what is right and positive about learners. ■ Make needed individual exceptions. ■ Provide guidance and support to learners. ■ Stand firm for human-centred values. ■ Organise learners and tasks harmoniously. ■ Appreciate the diversity and uniqueness of learners.
Feeling types	**How feeling types benefit from the natural inclination of thinking types to**
■ Need to pay attention to the details and logical implications of the task as well as to learners' emotional needs. ■ Need to learn how to value and manage conflict productively. ■ Need to recognise the limitations of learners and guard against unquestioning loyalty.	■ Analyse consequences and implications of decisions and goals. ■ Find the flaws in advance. ■ Uphold boundaries and classroom rules and policies consistently. ■ Give objective feedback to learners. ■ Stand firm for important principles and values.

- Need to detach self from carrying the mood and feelings of learners and learn to use objectivity in dealing with the general classroom mood.
- Need to suspend self-criticism and listen carefully to the objective information contained in feedback.
- Need to consider themselves personally when making decisions.

(Based on Myers, 1993)

- Be fair in exercising discipline.

Cyclical correspondences

Figure 7.2 shows the cyclical relationships between the six classroom conditions. Because they are located in the *emotional creativity cycle* there is a cyclical relationship between classroom psychological safety (condition 2) and purposeful behaviour (condition 5); positive self-image (condition 3) and personal competence (condition 6); teacher emotional intelligence profile (condition 1) and feelings of belonging (condition 4).

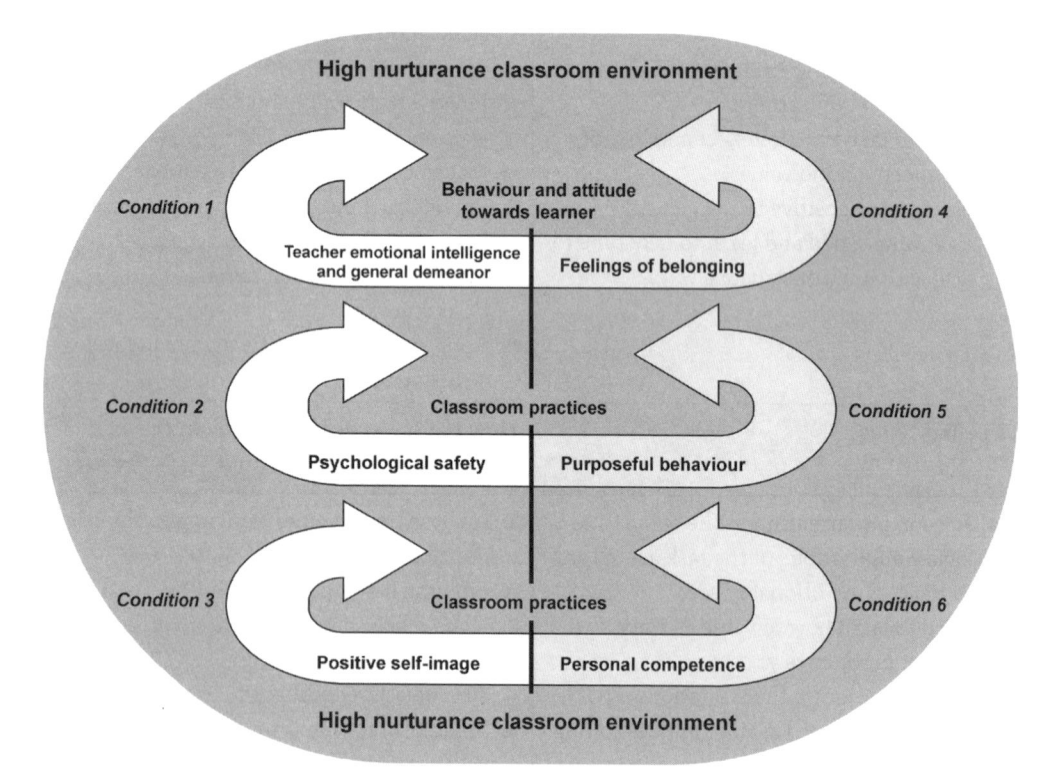

Figure 7.2 Cyclical correspondences between classroom conditions

Psychological safety and purposeful behaviour

When learners know clearly what is expected from them, they are apt to focus on goals and tasks. Learners are more willing to engage in purposeful behaviour when they are inspired by the intrinsic joy of learning and achieving realistic goals, and of solving their own problems. However, when learners are filled with anxiety and uncertainty they cannot concentrate on goals and learning tasks. Furthermore, if their efforts are directed towards pleasing or complying with the demands of the teacher, they will lack internal motivation.

Positive self-image and personal competence

Learners who have a positive self-image are apt to be confident about performing well. They have a sense of self-efficacy that enables them to attempt challenging goals and to persevere in their efforts. Feedback on their strengths and accomplishments facilitates a positive self-image and a sense of personal competence.

Learners who receive no or predominantly negative feedback about their abilities, generally lack the courage to attempt challenging tasks. They tend to have a low self-esteem which affects their sense of personal competence.

Teacher emotional intelligence profile and feelings of belonging

Emotionally intelligent teachers tend to display empathy towards learners. They treat them as equally important, yet recognise their uniqueness. They behave in a socially responsible manner towards learners and help them to feel motivated, inspired and proud to be part of the group. On the other hand, teachers who treat learners with disdain, impersonal coldness and impatience (lashing out in anger), make learners feel rejected. Learners then withdraw from classroom activities and may even lose respect for the teacher.

Table 7.3 Nine ways to motivate and inspire learners

Strategy	Reason
1. *Be motivated yourself.*	If teachers are enthusiastic, it is likely to rub off on learners.
2. *Each to their own.*	Each learner is different and will be motivated by different things. Teachers should find out what these are and use them.
3. *Give them a challenge.*	Goals should be realistic and achievable, yet challenging. Failure can be demotivating.
4. *Treat them with respect.*	Demonstrate to learners that you value them and their efforts. This is the bedrock of motivation.

5. *Listen to them.*	This implies more than just hearing what learners say, it involves understanding them and their views, thus showing empathy.
6. *Help them learn.*	Most children like learning something new, particularly if they think that it will be valuable to them.
7. *Welcome difficulties.*	Solving problems can be a challenge and interesting. This can motivate the learners if they perceive some benefit (a form of recognition or reward) as a result of solving a task-related problem.
8. *Recognition.*	Acknowledge the learners' contribution. Celebrate their successes.
9. *Raise the bar.*	Try to eliminate (or reduce) the frequency of repeating the same things every day. Set new, interesting and more difficult challenges to motivate learners and keep their interest and commitment.
(Based on Martin, 2005)	

It is useful to remember that if classroom conditions seem to be harder or easier for you, learners are likely to have an issue with the conditions directly across from it on the emotional creativity cycle. For instance, if you find that the condition personal competence/learners' performance causes you the most trouble (you may try to avoid it altogether), look at the opposite condition positive self-image/how learners think and feel about themselves. It is likely that learners experience the opposite condition most intensely.

If you gravitate towards a particular condition, identify what you like or what makes you feel competent in that condition. Discern whether you have the same or opposite skills in the corresponding condition. For example, you may be good at showing empathy, treating learners with respect and dignity, and ensuring that all feel unique. Yet you also treat everyone as equals and make sure that all learners are included in classroom activities and feel part of the team (conditions 1 and 4).

On the other hand, it may be difficult for you to lay down the rules, communicate your expectations to learners and get them motivated to set goals for themselves (conditions 2 and 5).

You may tend to believe in the learners' abilities, help them to recognise their strengths and talents, and help them identify challenging tasks. Yet you make an effort to provide feedback on their progress by bolstering their self-image (conditions 6 and 3).

Pinpointing the problem or favourite classroom conditions increases your ability to identify your own strengths and weaknesses. It gives you more control over the emotional climate in the classroom. Knowing your strengths and weaknesses, enables you to use them to your advantage, rather than feeling like a victim of classroom behaviour.

Learn to be flexible

Another important secret of successful teachers is flexibility. This is the tendency to change attitudes and behaviour in the context of adopting a totally and dramatic new approach to teaching. While you will have become more adaptable, it does not mean that you have mastered the art of flexibility. To master the skill of flexibility, two primary skills have to be practised every day: dealing with interruptions and flexible self-talk.

Deal resourcefully with interruptions

Flexibility is a form of fine tuning. At time it is both an art and a science. Flexibility is the resilience we show when little things disrupt our lives or the classroom routine and alter what we were expecting. These could be when:
- A learner is late for class.
- Learners walk into the classroom with an attitude of resistance.
- A schedule change in a busy day is made to accommodate a special arrangement by the principal.
- The principal unexpectedly drops in at your classroom.
- A learner ignores an instruction.
- Learners did not complete their homework.

The challenge is to recognise that these disruptions upset you emotionally and to quickly take steps to get back on track in an emotionally intelligent manner.

! Try this now!

Example

Interruption

A learner is late for class.

Solution

Breathe deeply to keep calm. Listen to the learner's apology and allow her to take her seat. Arrange with the learner to have a private discussion to discuss the reasons and consequences of her behaviour.

Interruption

Learners walk into the classroom with an attitude of resistance.

Solution

Interruption

A schedule change in a busy day is made to accommodate a special arrangement by the principal.

> **Solution**
>
> **Interruption**
> The principal unexpectedly drops in at your classroom.
> **Solution**
>
> **Interruption**
> A learner ignores an instruction.
> **Solution**
>
> **Interruption**
> Learners did not complete their homework.
> **Solution**

How you emotionally respond in a relationship – with joy, sadness, fear or anger – can say a lot about your thoughts and belief systems.
(Deepak Chopra)

Successful teachers thrive on flexibility and bend to make the alterations workable in a win/win way. That is why they remain happy, energetic and creative.

Practise flexible self-talk

Flexibility means having bend and flow for the purpose of creating resolve and forward movement. Unfortunately, many teachers go through the day resisting little changes and stand firmly against them. Keeping to the classroom routine is their only focus. By the time the week has passed, they are ready to explode with anger or frustration about all the interruptions. Resistance has the power to accumulate and fill us with stress.

The irony is that resisting and moving against little changes takes more energy than flowing with them. Stress comes from resistance. Ease comes from flowing with life and all it brings. Although, there are degrees of resistance, the goal is to embrace the little interruptions and alterations and create something useful and positive from them.

Table 7.4 depicts the flexibility self-talk of successful teachers as opposed to the self-talk of others. Negative self-talk can become a downward spiral that creates tremendous resistance and stress. Conversely, positive self-talk propels successful teachers to use their emotional creativity to find solutions and actions which release stress.

Table 7.4 Flexible self-talk

Successful teachers	Others
■ How can I make it work? ■ What is the advantage in this? ■ This might mean … (reframe to positive). ■ What is my emotional need right now? ■ I'll gather more information before responding. ■ I can be responsible for what to do now.	■ What problems does this create for me? ■ How does this take advantage of me? ■ This probably means … (assume negative/bad). ■ How can I protect myself? ■ React immediately. ■ "They" are responsible for ruining my day.

(Based on Brock and Salerno, 1994)

Teachers who wish to create classroom conditions that foster optimal learning and growth opportunities for their learners will find the Ten Day Plan to Excellence valuable.

Follow the Ten Day Plan to Excellence

- **Day 1:** Find new vision.
- **Day 2:** Foster psychological safety.
- **Day 3:** Explore the secret of wonderful feelings.
- **Day 4:** Build positive self-images.
- **Day 5:** Listen to the values of the heart.
- **Day 6:** Foster feelings of belonging.
- **Day 7:** Establish purposeful behaviour.
- **Day 8:** Foster personal competence.
- **Day 9:** Review your accomplishments.
- **Day 10:** It's a wonderful life … if you notice.

The Ten Day Plan to Excellence

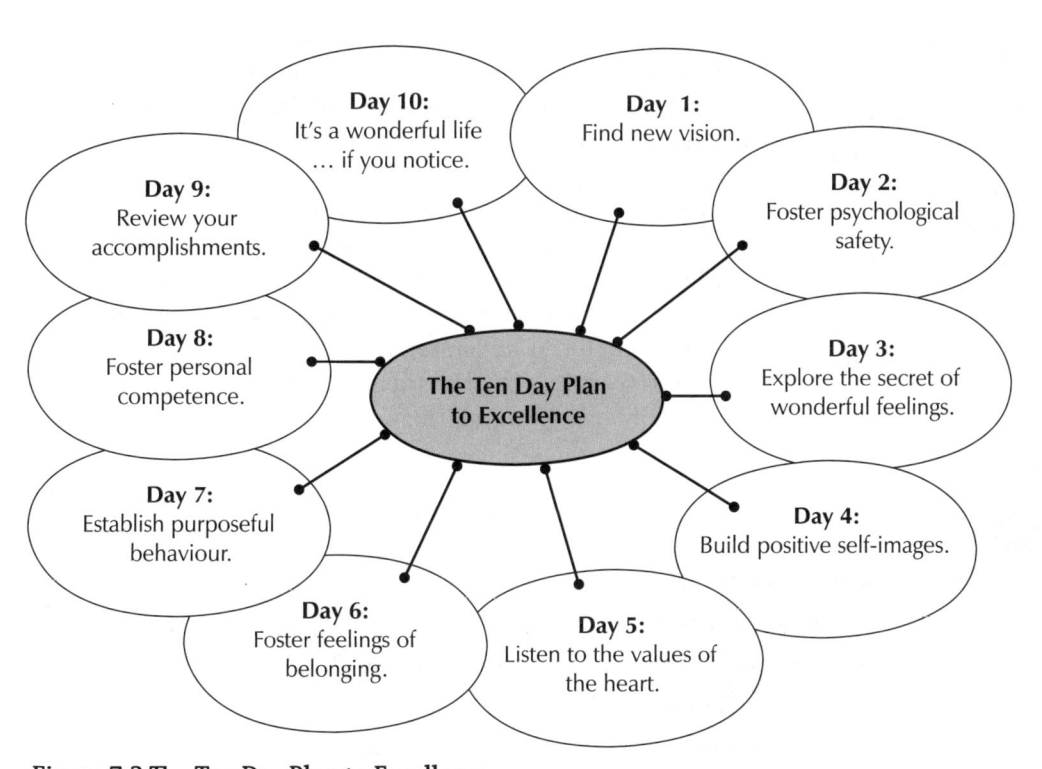

Figure 7.3 The Ten Day Plan to Excellence

Day 1 Find a new vision

Today, set aside time to reflect on your ideal self. Who would you like to become? Be willing to view yourself and your life from a new perspective. Many things in life reveal their qualities when perceived in the right way. Often familiarity makes it difficult for us to see the beauty in ourselves and others. Try to look at everything and everyone (especially yourself) with fresh eyes, unclouded by habit. This way you may discover untold riches.

We inadvertently adhere to behavioural patterns which we ourselves have created. If we repeat the same behaviour, we get the same results. In order to make progress, we need to break out of the confines of our regular, restrictive actions. In this way, we learn to make the changes that will set us free from our stress-inducing habits.

Learn to manage your feelings through good thoughts. Today, monitor your thoughts closely. When a negative thought creeps in, check yourself and substitute it with something positive. Discard and replace negative thoughts with positive ones. This helps us to send out benevolent emotions into the world. It draws back goodness into our lives.

Be grateful for the diversity that your learners offer you. Today, when you come across behaviour and viewpoints that are emotionally upsetting, try to see your learners as unique individuals. They all have an important contribution to make to life. Their viewpoints reflect the rich diversity of all creation. Remember, criticism generates discord, but tolerance and compassion create peace and harmony.

Finally, and most importantly, take time to value yourself: We feel liberated when we explore new aspects of ourselves, the hidden treasures that remind us of the riches of our being. Never fear to discover the bounty within yourself for it will encourage self-insight and self-understanding. When you become aware of these treasures, visualise them as often as you can. Direct your energy into bringing them to life.

Until today, you may have been holding on to secret thoughts and feelings. You may have been afraid to open yourself up to self-examination or outside scrutiny. Just for today, be willing to release those things stored in your heart and mind that are causing you discomfort. (Iyanla Vanzant)

Try this now!

Day 1 Find a new vision

1. My ideal self (vision): How I would like to be
2. My real self: Who I am (strengths, growth areas, blind spots)
3. New behavioural patterns I would like to practise
4. Development plan (actions I can take to develop my emotional intelligence)
5. Where will it be safe to experiment with the new behaviour?
6. What opportunities are available (in the classroom and at home) to practise the new behaviour?
7. Who do I trust enough to give me support and feedback on this journey, e.g. a coach, a counsellor, a mentor, a colleague or a partner?

Day 2 Foster psychological safety

Set the stage by reviewing with your learners the kind of classroom you would like to have. Ask them what is important to them and what behaviours they would like to see. Develop a list of characteristics that most of the learners would like to have in the classroom.

Use class meetings to discuss general classroom behaviour and discrepancies between the ideal classroom characteristics and what has actually been observed. Gain parental support in working for improvement.

Establish routines for things, such as entering and leaving the classroom, handing in and giving out papers, collecting and distributing materials or correcting papers. Make sure that procedures are well understood.

Develop individual behaviour contracts for learners who find it difficult to conform. Include in the contract the standards of expected behaviour, learner commitment to agreed standards, and the consequences of failing to meet standards.

Develop your own hypotheses regarding possible reasons for learner misbehaviour to determine what the benefit or advantage is to the learner. Then seek ways to help the learner meet his or her needs or desires in socially acceptable ways.

Set classroom standards to ensure that no learner is emotionally or physically abused by others. Recognise learners who demonstrate genuine effort to improve their behaviour. Provide a special reward, such as lunch with the teacher, a sweet treat, or the use of a special computer programme.

Work with learners who violate standards on a one-to-one basis. Whenever possible, avoid embarrassing them in front of their peers. This will reduce the likelihood of the learner using the incident as an opportunity to act up in front of the class.

Build trust by telling learners what is likely to happen. This way they can anticipate future events. Provide them with explanations for events they may have looked forward to but that did not occur.

! Try this now!

Day 2 Foster psychological safety
1. Ideal classroom
2. Ideal behaviours
3. Current behaviour
4. Important classroom routines
5. Reasons for learner misconduct
6. Important classroom standards
7. Ideas for special rewards
8. Ways to deal with violations
9. New behaviour I would like to display

Day 3 Explore the secret of wonderful feelings

Today, make it your secret task to encourage learners to feel better. Use a kind and sincere word, a gesture or a smile, an offer or a little gift. Innovate and create according to your circumstances. Write down your results at the end of the day. Continue with this for as long as you find it rewarding.

Apply it also to yourself. What emotion, if you could experience it several times a day, would make your life and teaching smoother and more wonderful? What three things could you do to unfold this emotion in yourself? Start today.

> **! Try this now!**
>
> **Day 3 Explore the secret of wonderful feelings**
> 1. Words of encouragement I gave today
>   Learner/words
> 2. Results
> 3. Emotion that would make my life/teaching smoother
> 4. Three things I could do to unfold this emotion in myself

Day 4 Build a positive self-image

Plan activities that provide learners with opportunities to explore different forms of art, music, crafts, collections and games. Encourage them to develop their own interests, talents and abilities.

Begin a compliment chain by giving one learner a compliment. Have that learner give another learner a compliment until every learner gains practise in giving a genuine compliment.

Develop with the class many ways of giving praise or recognition to individuals. This could include clapping, or giving a thumbs-up sign. Find out positive qualities about each learner that you can associate with them. Relate to learners in terms of their positive qualities rather than their negative ones.

Think of negative qualities as possible strengths for you to build on. For example, learners who demonstrate bossy behaviour could be exhibiting leadership, learners who demonstrate stubborn behaviour may be determined. Help learners to use their qualities appropriately.

Work with each learner and encourage him or her to distinguish those tasks or subjects that are difficult for them and those which are easy. Talk about ways they could use to compensate for the things that are difficult and how to overcome the problem.

Help learners identify and learn to express their feelings and moods. Play different kinds of music or talk about different experiences. Let them express their feelings and responses. Teach them vocabulary to help them verbalise their emotions. Make it a game to introduce new words to describe moods and feelings.

Recognise learners who deserve special attention. Show them how those who develop inner discipline overcome problems and grow up to be strong adults. Invite parents and other community members to share with learners the special work they do or to stimulate new interests.

> **! Try this now!**
>
> **Day 4 Build a positive self-image**
> 1. Unique qualities of my learners
>   Name/Unique quality
> 2. Activities that can help learners to discover their special abilities and talents
> 3. Ideas for genuine compliments
> 4. Ideas for giving praise/recognition
> 5. Positive qualities of learners
>   Name/Quality
> 6. Turning negative qualities into possible strengths
>   Negative quality, possible strength
> 7. Recognition ideas for learners

Day 5 Listen to the values of the heart

Today, practise listening and empathising skills. Hear and understand the heartfelt values of your learners. Listen for their goals. Repeat what you hear about what they say aloud to give them the opportunity to confirm or clarify your understanding. Ask them what is important about achieving their goals and values. When you do this you are asking for their deeper values, their heartfelt values. Listen as they tell you.

You may want to begin a file of heartfelt values for your learners, since these are the values they live for and that they seek to be fulfilled before they commit themselves to learning new tasks and setting new goals. Help your learners find ways to express their heartfelt values and thereby help them to set their talents free.

> **! Try this now!**
>
> **Day 5 Listen to the values of the heart**
> 1. Heartfelt values of learners
>   Learner/values
> 2. Talents learners may have (based on their values)
>   (Learner/values)

Day 6 Foster feelings of belonging

Develop a "Getting to Know You" chart that designates birthdays, birth places, pets, brothers and sisters, favourite games, hobbies and interests. The chart will show learners what they have in common.

Assign a buddy to each new learner. Have buddies interview new learners to gather information. Allow the buddies to introduce the newcomer to the class. Assign learners to co-operative learning groups so that they can bond with a small group of supportive learners.

Give all learners the opportunity to be an expert in something, for example, spelling, science or editing. Encourage learners to call upon the class experts whenever they need help in those areas.

Observe learners in your class to identify those who isolate themselves. Make a special effort to have them sit by others who will accept and include them. Work with learners who need special help in developing social skills. Let them see the impact of their behaviour on others. Teach them how to grow positive social relationships.

Use class meetings to address issues or concerns and to consider suggestions for improving the class. Set up committees to work on solutions. Follow up on their recommendations and report back to the class. Encourage learners to use respectful behaviour towards each other, to express thanks or appreciation for acts of kindness.

! Try this now!

Day 6 Foster feelings of belonging
1. Getting to know my learners
   Name/Important aspects to remember
2. Identify class experts
   Name/Expert
3. Identify isolates
   Name/Ideas to include him/her
4. Ideas for special projects to build group pride
5. Learners' suggestions for improving the class
6. Ideas for respectful behaviour

Day 7 Establish purposeful behaviour

Expose learners to the career fields they might want to consider. Have them research information on the training required, possible forms of employment available, and the reasons why people choose to work in these fields.

Ask learners to identify the values that are most important to them and the code of ethics they try to live by. Post mottos or quotations up the classroom to encourage learners to lead inspired lives. Change these every week. Learners could use the statements as a basis for writing assignments to define what the words of inspiration mean to them.

Reinforce the concept that your learners can achieve great things if they work towards their goals by taking one step at a time. Let learners set a major goal that they hope to accomplish by the end of the school year.

Stress how important is to develop lifelong learning habits and to establish a firm skills base upon to build. Encourage learners to reach for increasingly higher levels of proficiency. Stimulate goal setting by suggesting challenges that learners might want to take on their learning areas. Assure learners that you will provide the support they need to achieve their goals. Express confidence in their ability to achieve success.

> **! Try this now!**
>
> **Day 7 Establish purposeful behaviour**
> 1. Learners' career dreams
>   Name/Career dream
> 2. Important values
>   Name/Values
> 3. Special goals
>   Name/Goals
> 4. Message of confidence to my learners

Day 8 Foster personal competence

Allow learners to track their progress in different subject areas in a journal or log. They can record their accomplishments as the year progresses. Teach them how to use self-evaluation checklists, progress charts, graphs and portfolios.

Brainstorm with learners options they might consider to achieve their goals. Encourage them to select the option that might be the most effective for them. Periodically review the progress they are making in using the option they chose. Allow them to select a new option if the old one does not seem to be working.

When learners identify a goal, have them list the subskills required, the steps to be taken, and the hurdles to be overcome. When a crisis occurs, teach learners how to address it. Rather than solve the problem, help learners define the problem, examine the factors that contributed to the problem, explore possible ways of addressing it, as well as the alternatives, to determine which approach would be most effective.

Reward learners who need this to motivate them. When learners achieve a personal goal, review the knowledge they gained, the skills they learned, and the insights they had about themselves. Talk them about how to use this information to set a higher goal.

Teach learners how to use positive self-talk to encourage themselves when they work through problems. Demonstrate the use of self-talk.

Create a simple recognition ceremony at the end of the week for learners who have achieved their goals. Send home a note to their parents to let them know how successful their children have been.

> **Try this now!**
>
> **Day 8 Foster personal competence**
> 1. Options to achieve goals
>   Name/Goal/Options
> 2. Skills required to achieve goals
>   Name/Goal/Skills required
> 3. Possible words of encouragement
> 4. Possible barriers that may block learner progress
> 5. New skills learned
>   Name/Skills
> 6. Ideas for motivation rewards
> 7. Special achievements
>   Learner/Achievement
> 8. Ideas for a recognition/celebration ceremony

Day 9 Review your accomplishments

Today, take time to reflect on what you have accomplished during days 1 to 8. Celebrate your successes. Think of ways to sustain these new habits and practices.

Think about which the classroom conditions still need improvement. Write down possible reasons and solutions. Write down any new ideas for sustaining a positive emotional climate in the classroom. Involve your learners in the process.

> **Try this now!**
>
> **Day 9 Review your accomplishments**
> 1. New habits/practices
>   Habit/practice/effect on classroom climate
> 2. Ways to sustain the positive climate
> 3. Classroom conditions that need more attention
> 4. Ideas/solutions to improve these conditions

Day 10 It's a wonderful life, if you notice

On this day of rest, you might begin by congratulating yourself for having worked through this book and applying the ideas and practices in your life, and particularly in the classroom. We all make a difference in the lives of others, whether intentionally or unconsciously.

Take a few moments: In your mind's eye, go to your past and find small, as well as significant ways where you have affected the world of your learners positively. Perhaps you helped and supported them to master a challenging assignment, or gave an opinion that made all the difference. Seek out the times where you have touched their lives with your words and deeds. Make a list of the words and their effects, even if they were not obvious until years later. Sometimes the actions most valued by others are not the ones we value.

Expand your measuring stick to include how important you have been to your learners to include what is important to you. A nudge at the right time can make the difference. These experiences are proof of how important your everyday actions are. Take a few moments to write down actions you would like to take in future, actions that will add value to your learners' lives. As you write them down, rehearse how you will take these actions into the classroom. Enjoy your participation in making the world a wonderful place.

> **! Try this now!**
>
> **Day 10 It's a wonderful life, if you notice**
>
> 1. Words or actions taken
> 2. Positive effect on learners' lives
> 3. Actions I will take in the future

Make a commitment right now to take up the challenge to be a happy teacher. Consciously apply emotional intelligence to everyday situations. It will help you to increase your overall sense of well-being and be creative about your emotional and mental state.

Teachers who are in touch with their feelings and know how to negotiate their way through the many feelings life brings, have found the secret of inner peace and vitality that make up emotional health.

Celebrate your success;
Enjoy your discovery;
Grow in your insight!

Write down your goals. Review them at regular intervals to see what you would like to accomplish today, next week, within a month and by this time next year. Celebrate your success, you deserve it.

A Promise to Myself: A Commitment to Act!

Today I will

_____
_____
_____

This week I will

_____
_____
_____

Within a month I will

_____
_____
_____
_____
_____

By this time next year, I will

_____
_____
_____

Signed: **Date:**

In conclusion, embrace your emotional intelligence fully so as to inspire and motivate your learners to be the best they can. Mastering and applying emotional intelligence effectively requires daily practice. It demands the will and intention to improve our lives and conditions in the classroom. Be flexible, open and willing to embrace a new way of being. Honour and nurture yourself.

Achievement of Excellence

My Development Achievements

Date: _____

Action taken (i.e. courses/seminars completed; books/articles read; people spoken to; experience had, etc)

New knowledge gained

New skills acquired

New behaviours/practices established in classroom

Use your rational brain to balance your emotional brain so as to achieve excellence in your life and profession as a teacher. Do not let the presence of emotions in the classroom scare you. Instead, harness their energy to create those conditions that serve the highest good of all. Emotional intelligence skills are extremely effective. Anyone can master them. Just do it, because you can!

> **Taking action!**
>
> *Three suggestions for putting the ideas in this chapter into practice:*
>
> 1. *Do a thorough study of the Cycle of emotional creativity in the classroom.* Familiarise yourself with the different conditions and how they correspond. Find ways to assess your current behaviour and classroom practices. Identify those practices that you would like to gain or improve.
> 2. *Recognise the blocks* and stop destructive patterns immediately. Review the activities and suggestions in the previous chapters to assist you.
> 3. *Follow the Ten Day Plan to Excellence* and repeat it as needed to create successful attitudes and beliefs. Review your progress regularly and celebrate your accomplishments. You deserve it.

Review questions

1. What role does motivation play in developing emotional intelligence?
2. Explain the Ten Day Plan to Excellence. What will teachers who follow this plan achieve?
3. Explain the six conditions of emotional creativity in the classroom. What is the teacher's role in establishing these conditions? How will these conditions benefit learners and teachers?
4. What are the blocks to establishing the six conditions of emotional creativity in the classroom?
5. How can teachers become more flexible? Why is it important for teachers to develop flexibility? What role does personality preference play in developing flexibility? (Review chapter 4)

> **✓ In a snapshot**
>
> 1. Motivation is the key to developing emotional intelligence. We need to be committed and willing to improve our emotional intelligence.
> 2. Teachers must be knowledgeable and skillful in establishing and monitoring the six classroom conditions that affect the general classroom climate.
> 3. Frequent measurement of the classroom climate will help teachers to improve the learning and performance of the class.
> 4. Understanding how personality preferences influence flexibility will help us to stop destructive behavioural patterns. The Ten Day Plan to Excellence can help teachers foster behavioural patterns that create optimal conditions for learners' growth and performance.

Suggested reading

Branden, N. (1994) *Six Pillars of Self-esteem*. New York: Bantam

Goldsworthy, R. (2000) 'Designing instruction for emotional intelligence' *Educational Technology*, 40 (5): 43–48

Kruger, AG. & Van Schalkwyk, OJ. (1997) *Classroom Management*. Cape Town: Van Schaiks

Le Roux, R. & De Klerk, R. (2004) *Emotional Intelligence Workbook: The All-in-one Guide for Optimal Personal Growth!* Pretoria: Human & Rosseau

Mather, N. & Goldstein, S. (2001) *Learning Disabilities and Challenging Behaviours*. Illinois: Paul H. Brookes Publishing Co

Reasoner, RW. (1992) *Building Self-esteem in Elementary Schools*. Palo Alto, California: Consulting Psychologists Press

Appendix: The behavioural profile of effective teachers

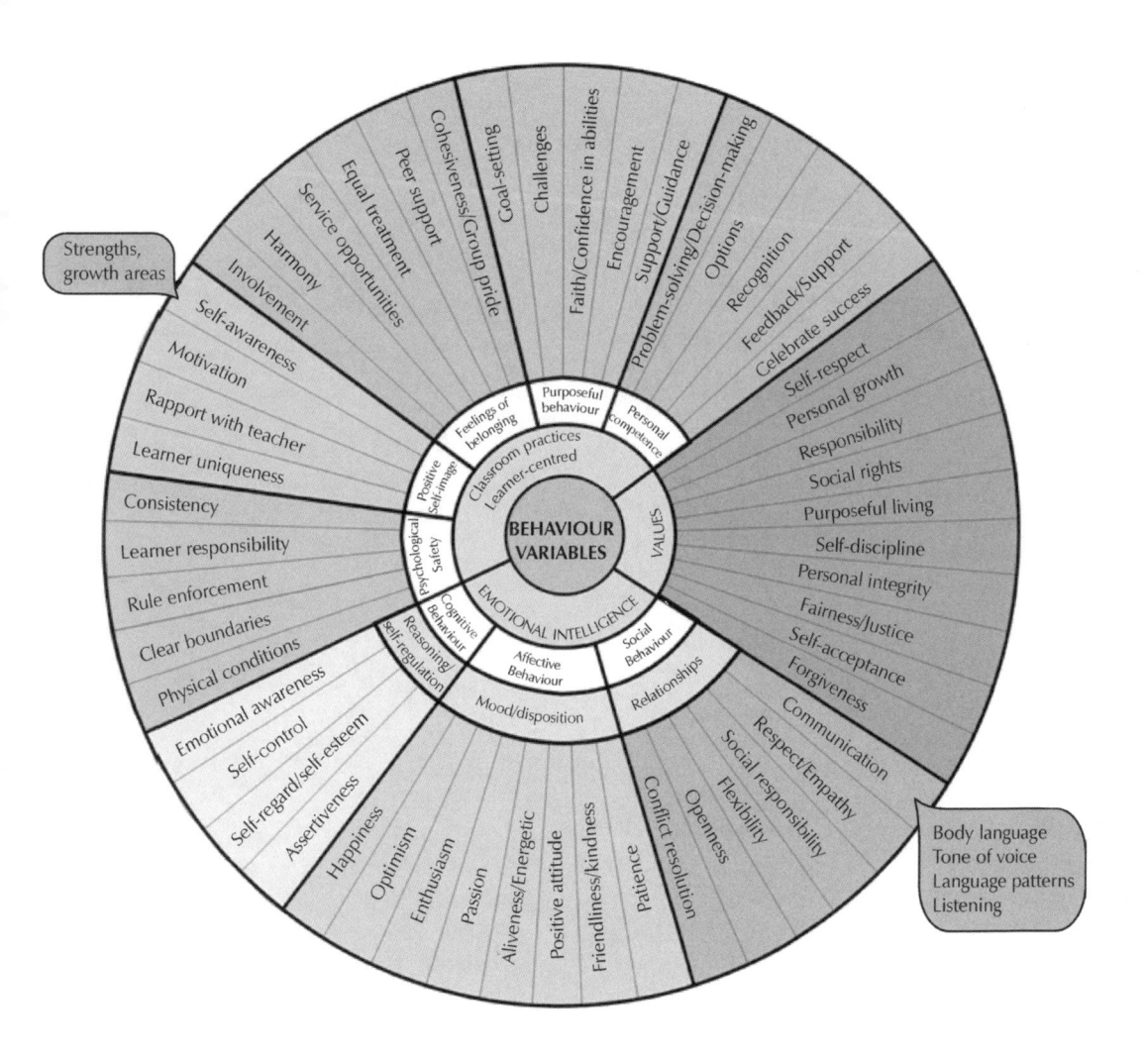

Strengths, growth areas

Body language / Tone of voice / Language patterns / Listening

BEHAVIOUR VARIABLES

Classroom practices — Learner-centred
- Purposeful behaviour
- Feelings of belonging
- Positive Self-image
- Psychological Safety

Inner ring segments
- Personal competence
- VALUES
- EMOTIONAL INTELLIGENCE
- Social Behaviour
- Affective Behaviour
- Cognitive Behaviour / Reasoning / Self-regulation

Outer ring labels (clockwise from top)
- Cohesiveness/Group pride
- Goal-setting
- Challenges
- Faith/Confidence in abilities
- Encouragement
- Support/Guidance
- Problem-solving/Decision-making
- Options
- Recognition
- Feedback/Support
- Celebrate success
- Self-respect
- Personal growth
- Responsibility
- Social rights
- Purposeful living
- Self-discipline
- Personal integrity
- Fairness/Justice
- Self-acceptance
- Forgiveness
- Communication
- Respect/Empathy
- Social responsibility
- Flexibility
- Openness
- Conflict resolution
- Patience
- Friendliness/kindness
- Positive attitude
- Aliveness/Energetic
- Passion
- Enthusiasm
- Optimism
- Happiness
- Assertiveness
- Self-regard/self-esteem
- Self-control
- Emotional awareness
- Mood/disposition
- Relationships
- Physical conditions
- Clear boundaries
- Rule enforcement
- Learner responsibility
- Consistency
- Learner uniqueness
- Rapport with teacher
- Motivation
- Self-awareness
- Involvement
- Harmony
- Service opportunities
- Equal treatment
- Peer support

Bibliography

Anderson, JA. & Mohr, WK. (2003) 'A developmental ecological perspective in systems of care for children with emotional disturbances and their families' *Education and Treatment of Children,* 26 (1): 52–74

Ashkanasy, NM. & Daus, CS. (2005) 'Rumors of the death of emotional intelligence in organizational behavior are vastly exaggerated' *Journal of Organizational Behavior,* 26: 441–452

Ashkanasy, NM., Härtel, CEJ. & Daus, CS. (2003) 'Diversity and emotion: The new frontiers in organizational behavior research' *Journal of Management,* 28 (3): 307–338

Bandura, A. (1997) *Self-efficacy in Changing Societies.* Cambridge: Cambridge University Press

Bar-On, R. (1997) *BarOn Emotional Quotient Inventory: A Measure of Emotional Intelligence – User's Manual.* Toronto, ON: Multi-Health Systems

Barth, JM., Dunlap, ST., Dane, H., Lochman, JE. & Well, KC. (2004) 'Classroom environment influences on aggression, peer relations, and academic focus' *Journal of School Psychology,* 42: 115–133

Bartholomew. (1987) *From the Heart of a Gentle Brother.* Carlsbad, CA: Hay House

Bell, J. (2003) *The Vital Factor in Healing,* Johannesburg: eB&W Publishing SA (Pty) Ltd

Biddulph, S. (1999) *The Secret of Happy Children.* New York: Harper-Collins

Bogdan, R. & Biklen, SK. (1998) *Qualitative Research for Education: An Introduction to Theory and Methods.* Boston: Allyn & Bacon

Branden, N. (1994) *Six Pillars of Self-esteem.* New York: Bantam

Brock, LR. & Salerno, MA. (1994) *The Inter-change Cycle: Managing Life Means Managing Change.* Dallas, Texas: Ussery Printing Company

Buckley, M., Storino, M. & Saarni, C. (2003) 'Promoting emotional competence in children and adolescents: Implications for school psychologists' *School Psychology Psychologist,* 18 (2): 177–191

Burney, R. (2006) Loving the Wounded Child Within. Retrieved from the Internet on 23 January 2006: http://www.joy2meu.com//innerchild.html

Cobb, CD. & Mayer, JD. (2000) 'Emotional intelligence: What the research says' *Educational Leadership*, 58 (3): 14–18

Coetzee, M. (2005) *The Relationship Between Personality Preferences, Self-esteem and Emotional Competence.* Unpublished DLitt et Phil (Industrial and Organisational Psychology) thesis. Pretoria: University of South Africa

Cummings, TG. & Worley, CG. (1993) *Organisation Development and Change.* New York: West Publishing

De Klerk, R. & Le Roux, R. (2004) *Emosionele Intelligensie.* Pretoria: Human & Rousseau

Denham, SA., Blair, KA., DeMulder, E., Levita, J., Sawyer, K., Auerbach-Major, S. & Queenan, P. (2003) 'Preschool emotional competence: Pathway to social competence?' *Child Development*, 74 (1): 238–256

Dyer, WW. (2004) *The Power of Intention.* London: Hay House

Elias, MJ. (2001) 'Easing transitions with social-emotional learning' *Principal Leadership*, 1 (7): 20–25

Epstein, R. (2000) *The Big Book of Stress Relief Games.* New York: McGraw-Hill

Ferrini, P. (1996) *The Silence of the Heart.* Greenfield, MA: Heartwayspress

Fineman, S. (2000) *Emotions in Organizations.* London: Sage

Fox, S. & Spector, PE. (2000) 'Relations of emotional intelligence, practical intelligence, general intelligence, and trait affectivity with interview outcomes: it's not just G' *Journal of Organizational Behavior*, 21: 203–220

Gerlach, PK. (2006) *Stepfamily in Formation.* Retrieved from the Internet on 23 January 2006: http://sfhelp.org/01/gwc-meaning.htm

Gerson, RF. (2000) 'The emotional side of performance improvement' *Performance Improvement*, 39 (8): 18–23

Goldsworthy, R. (2000) 'Designing instruction for emotional intelligence' *Educational Technology*, 40 (5): 43–48

Goleman, D. (2001) 'An EI-based theory of performance' in C. Cherniss & D. Goleman (editors) *The Emotionally Intelligent Workplace.* San Francisco: Jossey-Bass

Guralnik, DB. (editor) (1987) *Webster's New World Dictionary of the American Language.* Mexico: The World Publishing Company

Handron, DS., Dosser, DA., McCammon, SL. & Powel, JY. (1998) 'Wraparound –The wave of the future. Theoretical and professional practice implications for children and families with complex needs' *Journal of Family Nursing*, 4: 65–85

Hay, LL. (2004) *Everyday Positive Thinking.* Johannesburg: Hay House

Hirsh, S. & Kummerow, J. (1989) *Life Types.* New York: Warner Books

Jansen, CA. & Coetzee, M. (in press) *Emotional Intelligence and the Classroom Climate: A Behavioural Profile of the Educator*

Knitzer, J. (1996) 'The role of education in systems of care' in BA. Stroul (editor) *Children's Mental Health: Creating Systems of Care in a Changing Society.* Baltimore: Brookes

Kruger, AG. & Van Schalkwyk, OJ. (1997) *Classroom Management.* Cape Town: Van Schaiks

Landy, FJ. & Conte, JM. (2004) *Work in the 21st century.* New York: McGraw-Hill

Le Roux, R. & De Klerk, R. (2004) *Emotional Intelligence Workbook: The All-in-one Guide for Optimal Personal Growth!* Pretoria: Human & Rosseau

Lopes, PN., Brackett, MA., Nezlek, JB., Schutz, A., Sellin, I. & Salovey, P. (2004) 'Emotional intelligence and social interaction' *Personality and Social Psychology Bulletin,* 30 (8): 1018–1034

Martin, J. (2005) *Organisational Behaviour and Management.* United States: Thompson

Mather, N. & Goldstein, S. (2001) *Learning Disabilities and Challenging Behaviours.* Illinois: Paul H. Brookes Publishing Co

Mayer, JD. & Salovey, P. (1993) 'The intelligence of emotional intelligence' *Intelligence,* 17: 433–442

Mayer, JD. & Salovey, P. (1997) 'What is emotional intelligence: Implications for educators' in P. Salovey & D. Sluyter (editors) *Emotional Development, Emotional Literacy, and Emotional Intelligence: Educational Implications.* New York: Basic Books

Milanovich, N. & McCune, S. (1996) *The Light Shall Set You Free.* Albuquerque: Athena Publishing

Morris, E. (2002) 'Emotional literacy training for educators: Developing the whole person – linking hearts and minds in all learners' *Gifted Education International,* 16: 133–137

Mulligan, J. (1988) *The Personal Management Handbook: How to Make the Most of Your Potential.* London: Guild Publishing

Myers, IB., McCaulley, MH., Quenk, NL. & Hammer, AL. (1998) *MBTI Manual: A Guide to the Development and Use of the Myers-Briggs Type Indicator.* Palo Alto, California: Consulting Psychologists Press, Inc

Payne, JL. (2001) *Omni Reveals the Four Principles of Creation.* Florida: Findhorn Press

Preston, DL. (2005) *365 Ways To Be Your Own Life Coach.* Oxford: Howtobooks

Prevention (editors) (2004) *The Women's Health Bible.* London: Rodale

Quenk, NL. (1996) *In the Grip: Our Hidden Personality.* Palo Alto, CA: Consulting Psychologist Press

Reasoner, RW. (1992) *Building Self-esteem in Elementary Schools.* Palo Alto, California: Consulting Psychologists Press

Roman, S. (1988) *Personal Power through Awareness.* California: Kramer

Roman, S. (1989) *Spiritual Growth: Being Your Higher Self.* California: Kramer

Rothwell, WJ., Sullivan, R., & McLean, GN. (1995) *Practising Organisation Development*. Johannesburg: Pfeiffer & Company

Saarni, C. (1997) 'Emotional competence and self-regulation in childhood' in P. Salovey & DJ. Sluyter (editors) *Emotional Development and Emotional Intelligence: Educational Implications*. New York: Basic Books

Saarni, C. (1999) *The Development of Emotional Competence*. New York: Guilford

Salovey, P. & Mayer, JD. (1990) 'Emotional intelligence' *Imagination, Cognition, and Personality*, 9: 185–211

Salzberg, S. (2002) A heart as wide as the world. Retrieved from the Internet on 16 May 2002: http://innerself.com/Relationships/bridge of empathy.htm

Sterret, EA. (2000) *The Manager's Pocket Guide to Emotional Intelligence*. Amherst, MA: HRD Press

Tolle, E. (2001) *Practising the Power of Now*. London: Hodder & Stoughton

Trent, J. (1999) *Quiet Whispers from God's Heart*. Nashville, Tennessee: J. Countryman

Virtue, D. (1997) *Angel Therapy: Healing Messages for Every Area of Your Life*. California: Hay House

Walsch, ND. (2005) *What God Wants: A Compelling Answer to Humanity's Biggest Question*. London: Hodder Mobius

Glossary of terms

acceptance – to believe in another's worth and right to dignity; to approve of someone, irrespective of perceived strengths and shortcomings.
achievement – a facet of conscientious hard work, persistence and the desire to do good work.
affective behaviour – in the context of emotional intelligence, how you feel, including your mood and emotional state, how you use your emotions to be creative about your life and interactions; living from the heart.
anger – a feeling of displeasure and hostility resulting from injury, mistreatment or opposition.
anxiety – the state of being uneasy or worried about what may happen.
assertiveness – to be positive or confident in a persistent way that honours yourself and others.
attitude – a relatively stable feeling or belief directed towards specific persons, groups, ideas, tasks, behaviour or objects.
authenticity – to be open and honest; a term synonymous with the colloquial phrase "to be real" with someone.
authority – the power you have because of your official position; the teacher's right to insist on certain actions or behaviours from learners.
body language – an important part of non-verbal communication related to how thoughts, actions and feelings are transmitted through bodily movements and how other people interpret them.
burnout – the feeling of helplessness and of being unable to continue experienced after living under prolonged pressure.
classroom atmosphere – the general feeling or spirit (mood) of the classroom.
classroom climate – a shared perception amongst learners regarding a particular classroom or school, including how learners think and feel they are being treated by the teacher, thus creating a particular classroom atmosphere.
classroom environment – the conditions, circumstances and influences surrounding and affecting the development and

performance of learners, including the physical conditions of the school and classroom, the teacher's body language, physical appearance, language patterns, behaviour and attitudes towards learners.

cognitive ability – the capacity to reason, plan and solve problems; mental ability.

cognitive behaviour – in the context of emotional intelligence, how we think and reason about our feelings and emotions.

comforting connection – identifying an emotional need, underlying worry, hurt, anger or fear and using emotional creativity to fulfill that need.

commitment – internalisation of important values and norms underlying preferred behaviour; binding yourself to these by means of a promise or pledge.

communication – a process of sharing information and creating relationships in environments designed for manageable, goal-oriented behaviour, such as the classroom.

conflict – apparent disagreement between teacher and learners regarding a course of action, behaviour or values.

cycle of emotional creativity – an iterative approach to establishing high nurturance conditions in the classroom, thus leading to an emotionally warm classroom climate.

decision-making – a process by which a particular course of action is selected or a solution identified from amongst many options available.

depression – feelings of hopelessness and inadequacy.

development – formal education, experiences, guidance and support, personality assessments and abilities that help learners and teachers to improve their learning and performance.

dignity – the quality of being worthy of esteem and honour; a sound feeling of pride and self-respect.

dysfunctional behaviour – behaviour that is disruptive, non-compliant and that works against rules, standards and goals.

emotion – energy in motion; an expression of strong feelings about a thought; a mood or feeling, often experienced and displayed in reaction to an event or thought and accompanied by physiological changes in different systems of the body, often intense enough to disrupt thought processes.

emotional competencies – a unique set of competencies (knowledge, skills and attitudes) which enable us to manage our emotional life more effectively and successfully achieve our life goals, for example, emotional self-awareness, assertiveness, self-esteem, empathy, interpersonal skills, social responsibility, problem-solving, flexibility, stress tolerance, happiness and optimism.

emotional creativity – the ability to use your emotional state to create harmonious conditions and to achieve an inner sense of well-being and happiness.

emotional intelligence – an approach to intelligence which describes it in terms of the ability to perceive, to integrate, to understand and reflectively manage your own and other people's emotions; also, including the extent to which you are able to tap into your feelings and emotions as a source of energy to guide your thinking and actions; the ability to cognitively manage one's emotional life with greater or lesser skill.

emotionally cold classroom climate – a classroom climate characterised by coldness, inflexibility, impatience, punitive behaviour, embarrassment, belittling, disrespect, fear and anxiety, lack of pride, predominantly created by the teacher's behaviour towards learners.

emotionally warm classroom climate – a classroom climate characterised by emotional closeness, empathy, emotionally intelligent behaviour, respect and dignity, feelings of psychological safety and belonging, positive self-image, purposeful behaviour, a sense of personal competence and pride, predominantly created by the teacher's behaviour towards learners.

emotional self-awareness – understanding and being in touch with your feelings and emotions.

emotional wounds – the suppressed feelings of shame, rage, guilt, anger, fear, or sadness that are carried within, mostly caused by negative messages internalised or abuse suffered as children; false self wounds.

empathy – to be able to project yourself into another's feelings and hence to understand the other person; relatively interchangeable with sensitivity or understanding.

empowerment – when learners are given the freedom to take action (within clearly defined boundaries) without the need for specific approval.

encourage – to give courage, hope or confidence to a learner; to give support to a learner.

enthusiasm – intense or eager interest.

environment – the physical and social context within which a person, group or organisation, for example, a school, is functioning.

ethics – standards of acceptable behaviour for professionals practising in a particular field, such as education; in education, how teachers perform their helping relationship with learners; its focus is right, wrong, good and bad in relation to behaviour in the classroom context.

experience – direct participation in or observation of events and activities that serve as a basis for knowledge.

fairness – a value judgement about actions or decisions.

false self – the mask or front we present to the world to protect the True self; the adapted self.

fear – anxiety and agitation caused by the presence of danger, evil or pain; a feeling of uneasiness or apprehension; concern.

feedback – information regarding the actual performance or the results of the educational effort of a learner's performance; also, knowledge of the results of your actions that enhances performance.

feelings – thoughts and beliefs about someone or something; to be mentally aware of being, for example, to feel sad; to be moved, for example, to sympathy, compassion or anger.

feelings of belonging – feelings of connectedness to others and being part of something larger than yourself.

feeling type – a personality type that is sympathetic and interpersonally appreciative; a preference to base problem-solving and decision-making on human-centred values, thus creating harmony.

flexibility – the ability to adjust your emotions, feelings, thoughts and behaviour to changing situations and conditions.

forgiveness – the inclination to give up resentment against or the desire to punish.

goal-setting – a motivational approach in which specific, challenging goals direct learner attention and improve learner performance; also, activities that involve learners and teachers jointly when setting learning performance goals; monitoring these and providing encouragement, guidance and support when necessary.

Grown Wounded Child – adults who have survived unintended emotional and spiritual deprivation by their parents, teachers or caregivers.

guidance – advice or assistance given to learners by teachers.

guilt – a feeling of self-reproach resulting from the belief that what you have done is wrong or immoral.

happiness – a general feeling of cheerfulness and enthusiasm.

happy teacher – a teacher who has, shows or causes feelings of pleasure or joy in learners.

high nurturance environment – an environment that provides for childhood development needs, particularly emotional and spiritual needs.

impatience – behaviour that reflects intolerance and frustration resulting from being slowed down.

inner child – the child within the grown adult who has not recovered from childhood deprivation of basic development and emotional-spiritual needs.

inner critic – an inner voice that is given to faultfinding and censure; thoughts in the mind that form and express judgements of self and other people.

inner voice – an expressed wish, choice, opinion in the mind that influences judgement or behaviour; also, the voice of conscience causing feelings of guilt or shame for behaviour.

integrity – the quality of being honest, reliable and ethical.

intelligence – the ability to learn and adapt to an environment; often refers to general intellectual capacity, as opposed to cognitive ability or mental ability which are regarded as more specific memory or reasoning abilities.

interests – preferences or likings for a broad range of activities.

interpersonal competence – social awareness and social skills, such as the ability to resolve conflict and foster a spirit of co-operation.

interpersonal justice – justice that focuses on respectfulness and personal tone in communications surrounding the evaluation of learner performance and behaviour.

interpersonal relations – the connections between or amongst persons and groups, for example, the teacher and learners; the ability to establish mutually satisfying relationships.

love – goodwill and kindness towards others; opening your heart and mind to others; accepting them unconditionally.

low nurturance environment – an environment that deprives individuals of childhood development needs, particularly emotional and spiritual needs.

mood – a generalised state of feeling not identified with a particular stimulus and not sufficiently intense to interrupt ongoing thought processes.

mood awareness – being conscious of, knowing or realising a mental-emotional state.

motivation – a driving force that encourages individuals to behave in particular ways as they seek to achieve a goal; the willingness or energy with which individuals perform their tasks.

need – an internal motivation that is thought to be inborn and universally present in humans; also, a central concept in psychology, referring to a biological or psychological (emotional) requirement for the maintenance and growth of humans. It is used amongst educators primarily to refer to an emotional nurturance demand not met in the classroom environment, with the emphasis on the search for behaviours and practices that will facilitate the fulfillment of these needs.

negotiation – broadly reflects a process of difference reduction through forming agreements between learners and teachers who have mutually dependent needs and desires.

non-compliant behaviour – the disruptive behaviour of learners who do not follow classroom rules.

openness – accepting communications and confrontations of others, while expressing yourself honestly and authentically.

optimism – the tendency to take the most hopeful or cheerful view of matters.

passion – a strong love or affection; showing strong emotions.

performance – the level of achievement by a learner or a teacher, measured against what they would be expected to achieve.

personal competence – the accomplishment of personal goals and recognition received for achievements.

personality – an individual's behavioural and emotional characteristics, generally found to be stable over time and in a variety of circumstances; an individual's habitual way of responding.

problem-solving – the ability to confront and approach problems in a conscientious, disciplined, methodical and systematic manner.

projection – a psychological process of projecting onto others characteristics that we see in ourselves.

psychological safety – an emotional development need fulfilled by conditions, such as clearly identified classroom procedures, policies, rules and practices that reduce learners' anxieties. It includes physical conditions, such as neatness and cleanliness in the classroom and the availability of learning resources and equipment.

purposeful behaviour – the confidence and motivation to strive for personal achievable goals.

recovery – a return to mental-emotional and physical health by processing and releasing suppressed feelings; recovering from childhood wounds.

respect – to hold in high regard; to show honour or courtesy; consideration for others.

role model – someone who is identified as a person with the desirable qualities and values to be emulated by others.

self-absorption – a preoccupation with your own interests, needs and affairs.

self-acceptance – the belief in your own worth and right to dignity; to approve of yourself, irrespective of perceived strengths and shortcomings.

self-assertion – the act of demanding recognition for yourself or of insisting upon your rights.

self-awareness – becoming aware of your existing patterns of behaviour in a way that permits a relatively non-defensive comparison of those patterns with potential new ones.

self-confidence – confidence in yourself and your own abilities.

self-control – control of yourself, your emotions, desires and actions.

self-discipline – taking control of yourself, your emotional-mental state, attitudes and actions.

self-doubt – lack of self-confidence.

self-efficacy – the belief in your capability to perform a specific task or reach a specific goal; also, the belief that you can overcome obstacles and accomplish difficult tasks.

self-esteem – a positive self-worth or self-concept that is an important resource for emotionally intelligent behaviour.

self-image – your concept of yourself and your identity, abilities and worth.

self-respect – a proper respect for yourself and your worth as a person.

self-sabotage – intentional, deliberate damage to or obstruction of your efforts by your own self, often because you doubt your own worth or abilities.

shame – a painful feeling of having lost the respect of others because of improper behaviour or incompetence.

social behaviour – in the context of emotional intelligence, the response to and interaction with others as a result of the cognitive and affective aspects of emotional intelligence; also, balancing the rational and emotional brain to achieve inner harmony and well-being; to be open and flexible towards others.

social responsibility – the ability to act in a responsible, ethical manner; having a social conscience and a basic concern for the welfare of others.

stress – the non-specific response of the human body to any demand made on it; also, mental or physical tension or strain caused by urgency or pressure.

stress tolerance – the ability to withstand adverse events and stressful situations, without falling apart.

thinking type – a personality preference that uses impersonal logic and rationality when solving problems and making decisions.

True self – your talented, innocent self; your inner spirit; the Self that is not anxious or wounded; your seed of potential.

values – relatively permanent ideals (or ideas) that influence and shape the general nature of people's behaviour.

wounded child – a person who has suffered hurt to his or her feelings and honour as a young child; also, internalised negative messages received from parents, teachers or caregivers that have damaged your self-esteem and self-image and that are still carried within as an adult.

Index

Note: Page numbers in **bold** refer to concepts explained in the Glossary, and page numbers in *italics* refer to Tables and Figures.

A
abandonment 78
abilities of learners 5, 126
abuse 78
acceptance **99**–100
accomplishments, review
  of 130
acetylcholine 101
achievement **8**
acknowledgement
  of emotions 67, 70
  of inner critic 86
  of mistakes 100
adapted self, *see* false self
adaptive responses 55–57
addictions 104
adrenalin 93
affective representation 57
affective self-presentation
  38
affiliative values 39
allowing, state of 19
anger 5, 16, 18, 21, 23, 76,
  90–91, 103–104
anxiety 18, 23, 105–106
assertiveness 50, 51
attitude **2**, 3, 18
authencitity **56**
authority 53

B
balancing of emotions 99
behaviour
  generating of new 87
  impact of 71
  management 70–72
  patterns 57

behavioural preferences 110,
  114–115
behavioural profile
  affective dimension 54
  cognitive dimension 53
  effective teachers *135*
  social dimension 54–56

behavioural style 34–38
  impact on classroom
    climate *38*
  warm and cold *37*
belonging, feelings of **30**, 31,
  33, 35, 57, 118, 119
  fostering of 128
birth emotion 17
body language **27**, 35, 43,
  44
  and cultures 45
  reading of *44*
boundaries
  clearly defined 3, 4
  limits 71
brain
  chemistry 14–15
  stem 14
brainstorming 129
burnout 94–95

C
calm response 98
childhood wounds 76, 79
  recovery from 80–82
classroom
  conditions 120
  environment **30**, 32
  physical conditions 32,
    35

  rules 32
classroom atmosphere
  16–17, 18, 25, 30
  blind spots in sensing
    26–27
  energy 23
classroom climate **3**, 5, 23,
  30, 34–36, **36**
  emotionally cold 18
  emotionally warm 8, 30,
    33, 50, 56
  impact of teacher's
    behaviour 55–57, *57*
cognitive responses 15
cognitive self-presentation
  38
comforting connections
  96–97
commitment **32**, 125, 131,
  132
communication 43
  skills **2**–3, 4, 44
compassion 3, 18, 27–28, 56
competence, sense of 57
compliment chain 126
compromise 71
confidence 4
conflict **70**
cortisol 93
creativity, emotional **110**,
  113
  cycle of *114*
critical voice 85–86
criticism 84
cyclical correspondences
  118–120
  between classroom
    conditions *118*

D

decision-making **3**, 4, 116
demeanour of teacher 34–36
depression **18**, 21–22, 95
deprivation, unintended 78
desire to learn 31
destructive internal
    messages 85–87
development 117
    emotional 4
    potential areas of
    117–118
dialogue 71
differentiating between
    emotions 67
difficult learner behaviour
    70–72
dignity **30**
disagreements 70
discipline 5, 37, 53, 56, 70
diversity 124
dopamine 101
doubt 18, 23
dysfunctional family 31
dysfunctional vs
    emotionally intelligent
    responses *46*

E

emotion **6**, 12–15, 19
    managing of 4, 66, 71
    suppressing 66
emotional climate,
    monitoring of 115–116
Emotional Climate
    Sensor™ 34, 116
emotional competencies **50**,
    51–52
emotional connection 28
emotional creativity cycle
    118
emotional environment 4
emotional intelligence **1–2**
    assessing 62
    meaning of 49–51
    profile 118, 119–120
    teaching with 3–8
emotionally intelligent
    responses 66–67
emotional literacy 8
emotional needs **31**, 94, 95
emotional signals 14

emotional wounds **76**, 78
empathy **3**, 4, 26–27, 34,
    50, 51, 55
empowerment 4, 56
encouragement **3**, 34
enthusiasm **18**, 34
entitlement 5
environment **4**
equilibrium 60, 61
ethics **39**
expectations 22, 94
    of others 77
    realistic 33
experience **16**

F

fairness/justice **39**
false (adapted) self *76*,
    76–77
    dominance 79–80
    implications for teachers
    88–90
    wounds 79
fear **5**, 16, 18, 20–21, 23, 76,
    103, 105–106
fear-based feelings 5, 95
feedback 32, 34, 119
    verbal and non-verbal 44
feelings **6**, 13–14
    choosing of 16
    of connectedness 34
    of isolation 33
    tone 17
feeling type **58**, *59*, 61, 94,
    101, 116
flexibility **50**, 52, 121, 122
food and stress 101
forgiveness 21, 39
    parents or caregivers 81
frustration 21

G

genuineness 3,4
goals **8**, 33, 71, 119, 129,
    132
gratitude 18
group
    dialogue 71
    members of 33
    pride 33
Grown Wounded Child **77**,
    78–79

guidance **56**
guilt **18**, 21, 76, 103,
    106–108

H

habits 14
happiness **19**, 50, 52
    anxiety 22–24
    secrets of *19*
happy teacher 12, 25
    characteristics **2–3**
healthy connections 27
helplessness 21–22
high nurturance
    environment
high self-esteem 6–8
    traits 8
humiliation 104
humour 91
hurt 21, 76, 106–108

I

identity, sense of 57
impatience **5**
individual behaviour
    contracts 125
inferiority feelings 27
information 13
initiative 33, 34
inner child **77**, 90
inner critic **84**–90, 106
inner reality 13, 16
inner voice **84**–90
integrity **8**
intelligence **49**
intelligent reasoning 38
interests **126**, 127
interpersonal competence
interpersonal justice
interpersonal relations 24,
    50, 54
interruptions, dealing with
    121
IQ (general intelligence) 49
isolation, feelings of 33, 56

J

jealousy 16, 103
joy 16, 18
    of learning 33

Index

K
knowledge, reasons for acquiring 31

L
Law of Vibration 23–24
learner
   difficult behaviour 70–72
   misbehaviour 125
lifelong learning habits 129
limbic stress 95
limbic system (emotional brain) 14, 15, 95
listening
   to body 97
   skills 127
logic and rationality
   impersonal 58
   person-centred values-based 58
love **16**, 18–19, 106
low self-esteem 5–6
   traits 8

M
memories 15
mood awareness **13**, 44
morals 34
moral superiority 81
motivation 33, 34, 110–113
   and inspiration of learners *119–120*

N
negative emotions 18, 103
negative energy 25
negative self-evaluation 84
negotiation **86**
neocortex (rational brain) 14, 15, 60
neurons 15
neurotransmitters 101
non-compliant behaviour **70**
non-judgemental space 89
non-verbal behavioural cues 44
norepinephrine 93, 101
Now (present moment) 15–17
nurturance
   deprivations 78
   early needs 75

O
openness 8
open-heartedness 89
optimism **2**, 18, 50, 52
options 34
outer experience 16
outside reality 21
owning emotions 67

P
passion **3**, 34
peer conflict 57
peptides 15, 101
performance **43**
perseverance 7
personal competence **30**, 31, 34, 35, 118, 119
   fostering of 129
personal goals 33
personal growth 27, 39
personal integrity 39
personality preferences **66**, 94
   overuse of 116
personal management style 3
personal values 30
   statement *43*
personal worth 32
perspective 26
physical appearance 35
physiological response 66
pleasure and pain 16
positive leaning environment 30
positive emotions 18
positive self-esteem 33, 56
positive self-image 32–33, 34, 35, 56, 118, 119
potential 4, 34, 75
praise 126
preference 58–59
   overusing of 60–61
   thinking and feeling 58–59, *59*
   see also behavioural preferences
pride 3, 21, 33, 56
principle of resonance 25
problematic learner behaviour 70
problem-solving **38**, 50, 51, 55–57, 95, 116–117
projection **52**, 90, 105
psychological safety **30**, 31–32, 35, 119, 125
punishment 21
purpose, sense of 57
purposeful behaviour 30, 31, 33, 35, 118, 119
   fostering of 128–129
purposeful living 39

R
rapport 33, 35, 57
rational brain, *see* neocortex
rational self-talk 67
recognition 35, 126
recovery 80–83
   journey to 84
relationships 2–3, 52–53
   learners 115, *115*
   skills 2
remorse 105, 106
reporting emotions 67
resistance 122
resolution 67
respect **3**, 4, 34
responsibility 8, 33, 39, 81
reward 130
rights of learners 6
role model **32**, 105
routine 125

S
sadness 16, 18, 21, 103
safe space 4
satellite emotions 17
security, sense of 57
self-absorption **28**
self-acceptance **39**
self-awareness **4**, 6, 38, 50, 51
self-concept 22, 32
self-confidence
self-control **50**
self-discipline **39**
self-esteem **4**, 5–7, 30, 52–53
   characteristics 9–10
self-estimate 7
self-expression 21
self-fulfilling prophecy 22

self-image **31**, 126–127
self-judgement 84
self-regard 50, 51
self-respect **6**, 19, 32, 39, 56
   lack of 7
self-sabotage **22**
self-talk
   demonstrate use of 130
   flexible 122–123, *123*
   rational 67
self-worth 56
senses 13, 14
serotonin 101
shame 21, 76, **103**, 104–105
social behaviour **26**
social dimension 54–56
social interaction 26, 56, 60
social management skills 4
social responsibility **50**, 51, 56
social rights 39
social skills 3
socio-emotional climate 56
Spirit within us, *see* true Self
standards 34, 125
steroids 101
strengths and weaknesses 33, 81

stress **78**, 93
   hormones 93–94
   physical symptoms 98
   response 94–100
   tolerance 50, 52
   triggers 94–95
stress-free food 101
success, achievement of 34
superiority feelings 27
support 34, 56
   emotional 76
   parental 125
suppressed emotions 89, 103
   release of 103–108

T
talents 126
Ten Day Plan to Excellence *123*, 123–132
Think-Feel-Act-Have 22
thinking responses, *see* cognitive responses
thinking type **58**, 59, 61, 94, 101, 116
thoughts brushed with feeling 13, *13*
time out 67
True self **75**

acceptance of 82
and false self *76*
trust 82, 90, 125

U
unconditional aceptance 34
unconditional love 18–19
understanding of self 57–59, 110
uniqueness 33, 55, 56

V
value(s) **30**, 71
   of the heart 127
   modelling of 5
   system 66, 94
vibrations of energy 23–24
victimhood 81–82
vision 123–124

W
withdrawal behaviour 43
words, power of 43
worthiness 19–20
wounded childhood
   caregivers 79–80
wounded inner child **77**
   attributes of 77
   recovery 80–82, 84
wounded false self 76–77